ROBERT MURRAY M'CHEYNE

A GOOD MINISTER OF JESUS CHRIST

J. C. SMITH

AMBASSADOR

BELFAST ◆ GREENVILLE
NORTHERN IRELAND   SOUTH CAROLINA

Robert Murray M'Cheyne
A Good Minister of Jesus Christ

First published 1870
This edition Copyright © 1998 Ambassador Productions Ltd.

ISBN   1 84030 018 3

AMBASSADOR PRODUCTIONS LTD,
Providence House
16 Hillview Avenue,
Belfast, BT5 6JR
Northern Ireland

Emerald House,
1 Chick Springs Road, Suite 206
Greenville,
South Carolina 29609
United States of America

APPRECIATIONS

'He preached with eternity stamped upon his brow. I think I yet can see his seraphic countenance, and hear his sweet and tender voice. I was spellbound and would not keep my eyes off him for a moment. He announced his text - Paul's thorn in the flesh. What a sermon! I trembled, and never felt God so near. His appeals went to my heart, and, as he spoke of the last great day in the darkening twilight, for once I began to pray.'

Duncan Matheson

'All who knew him not only saw in him a burning and shining light, but felt also the breathing of the hidden life of God.'

Andrew Bonar

'My debt to McCheyne is continuous and increasing. His sanctity, his prayerfulness, his love of the Lord God, his passion for Jesus, his rich spiritual insight, make him a Prince in Israel.'

Dinsdale T. Young

'I have much enjoyed reading this book. Oh that we could have more of the spirit of McCheyne, and see again the work of those days.'

F. B. Meyer

ROBERT MURRAY M'CHEYNE

I

I WAS a boy, scarcely in my teens, when a blessed revival of religion broke out in St. Peter's Church, Dundee, in August 1839, during the pastorate of the late Rev. Robert Murray M'Cheyne, a name now well known and had in the greatest reverence and esteem throughout the whole Christian world. He valued the Bible very much, and said, "One gem from that ocean is worth all the pebbles of earthly streams." And he wrote in his diary about this time: "Lord, what a happy season is a Sabbath evening! What will heaven be? Oh, how sweet to work all day for God, and then to lie down at night under His smiles."

There were no displays of eloquence, but very marked outpourings of the Holy Spirit on numerous souls, to their awakening and conversion to God.

He was now sent by the Church of Scotland as one of a deputation to the Jews in Palestine; and a young preacher of the Gospel, named William C. Burns, was left in charge of the congregation, to whom Mr. M'Cheyne wrote a letter of farewell, and added: "It is said of the Rev. John Welsh, the minister of Ayr, that he used always to sleep with a plaid upon his bed, that he might wrap it round him when he arose in the night to pray. He used to spend whole nights wrestling with God for Zion and for the purity of the Church of Scotland. When God puts it into the hearts of His children to pray, it is certain that He is going to pour down His Spirit in abundance."

It was about the month of August 1839 when the great work of revival began in Dundee. The Spirit was indeed poured out in abundance, and the Word of God came "in power and in the Holy Ghost, and in much assurance" (1 Thess. i. 5). The hearts and consciences of the people were stirred to their very depths, and large congregations filled St. Peter's Church nearly night after night, many being under serious concern about the salvation of their souls, with deep convictions of sin; and numbers of them began to see themselves as lost sinners in the sight of a holy God. Their anguish and fear under these impressions were so great that they were fain, like Christian in Bunyan's *Pilgrim's Progress*, to break out into a lamentable cry, saying, "What must I do to be saved?" Many listened and responded to the earnest cry of the preacher to believe and live.

> " They had the Bible. Hast thou
> Ever heard of such a book?
> The Author, God Himself. Most
> Wondrous book. Bright candle

> "Of the Lord—star of eternity! the
> Only star by which the bark of
> Man could navigate the sea of life,
> And gain the coast of bliss."—POLLOK.

The work of grace was great, and spread to the neighbouring parishes, with deep conviction of sin, and in numberless cases with gracious manifestations of the way of salvation, through faith in the Saviour the Lord Jesus Christ.

A large number of private meetings were also held in the town; as many as thirty-nine were held weekly. The boys and girls were not overlooked, and the spirit of prayer was poured into their young hearts, so that five meetings were attended by, and entirely conducted by, young people in those bright and lovely days.

Time after time we would meet together to read the Bible and sing and pray. There were some verses which were favourites with us, and we would often sing them together—I suppose perhaps for our comfort and testimony; because some of the boys and girls who were not affected by the revival may not have been very friendly with us. The 54th Paraphrase was a great favourite, namely—

> "I'm not ashamed to own my Lord,
> Or to defend His cause,
> Maintain the glory of His cross,
> And honour all His laws.

> "Jesus, my Lord! I know His name,
> His name is all my boast;
> Nor will He put my soul to shame,
> Nor let my hope be lost.

"I know that safe with Him remains,
Protected by His power,
What I've committed to His trust
Till the decisive hour.

"Then will He own His servant's name
Before His Father's face,
And in the New Jerusalem
Appoint my soul a place."

The earnest prayers of Mr. M'Cheyne for his flock were indeed graciously and mightily answered by the Holy Ghost being poured out on His young servant in charge, Rev. William C. Burns. "Scarcely had Mr. Burns," wrote one, "entered on his work in St. Peter's when his power as a preacher began to be felt. Crowds flocked to St. Peter's from all the country round, and the strength of the preacher seemed to grow with the incessant demands made upon it. Wherever Mr. Burns preached, a deep impression was produced on his audience, and it was felt to be impossible to remain unconcerned under the impassioned earnestness of his appeals."

"Read the Bible for your own growth first," wrote Mr. M'Cheyne to his young assistant in St. Peter's, "then for your people. Expound much. It is through the Truth that souls are to be sanctified, not through essays upon the Truth. Be of good courage; there remaineth much of the land to be possessed. My dear people are anxiously waiting for you. The prayerful are praying for you. I shall hope to hear from you when I am away. Your accounts of my people will be a good word to make my heart glad. I am often sore cast down, but the Eternal God is my refuge. Now farewell; the Lord make you a faithful steward."

When Mr. M'Cheyne returned to Dundee from Palestine, he requested to be furnished with some particulars of the work of God going on in the town. It was arranged that a boy named Tom Brown and I were to call on him with information about our meetings of boys and girls. When we called at his house a servant took us into the kitchen, went across the lobby and knocked at the minister's door. He came to us wearing a dark dressing-gown, and received our paper; but I cannot recollect any more— perhaps the excitement had driven the remainder of the interview out of my mind. Happy early days!

But they are not lost; their memory remains, although most of my companions of these times have passed away.

There are calls to mourn over personal defections and falls, yet the blood of sprinkling applied, has washed all these vile stains away—praise the Lord! The Bible is nicely adapted for the young, and we then read it and loved it and believed it from board to board, as I do yet.

> "O children, hither do ye come,
>   And unto me give ear;
> I shall you teach to understand
>   How ye the Lord should fear."
>
> *Psalm* xxxiv. 11.

And the Bible is also very well adapted to the aged believer, so as to soothe and smooth his passage in life's pilgrimage during his declining years. And then what do we read to him who, as his eyes are dimming in death and the Master's chariot is on its way to carry him to the home beyond the flood? Just the same old words which we read or sang in our young days, which are ever fresh and ever new— " Let not your heart be troubled : ye believe in God, believe also in Me. In My Father's house are many mansions: if it were not so, I would have told you. I go to prepare a place for you. And if I go and prepare a place for you, I will come again, and receive you unto Myself; that where I am, there ye may be also" (John xiv. 1–3).

> "I go your entrance to secure,
> And your abode prepare :
> Regions unknown are safe to you,
> When I, your Friend, am there."
>
> *Paraphrase* xiii. 3.

We may well long for true revivals of religion when we read in Mr. Robe's narrative of former revivals as follows: "The moral influence on the parish generally was remarkable; visible reformation from many open sins, particularly cursing, swearing, and drinking. The worship of God is set up and maintained in many families who formerly neglected it. Former feuds and animosities are in a great measure laid aside and forgot," etc. etc. We may well pray, after the above gracious work—

> "Revive and quicken us, O Lord,
> Even for Thine own name's sake."
>
> *Psalm* cxliii. 11.

This true revival has been a lasting one also to some of my friends, as the 11th Paraphrase has it—

> "And who celestial Wisdom makes
> His early, ONLY choice."

An aged lady writes me, with thanks for my kind remembrance of her beloved minister, Mr. M'Cheyne, "who being dead yet speaketh." She says: "I was only seventeen years of age then; to-day I am eighty-four, and his voice is as clear and sweet as ever, and his teaching has been profitable to me, has remained as the rule of my life all these long years. Often have I thanked the Lord, that brought me to Christ. Chosen not for good in me, in those days under such a holy man, for I have never heard preaching which had the same power over me since. I pray you may be long spared to spread abroad Christ's Glorious Name."

And my dear aged friend, the Rev. John Duke, who himself was deeply engaged in revivals, as I recollect, is pleased to hear these memories of Mr. M'Cheyne, and writes me as follows: "It always affords me great delight to read any record of the revival of the Lord's work. Joy fills my heart as I call to remembrance special times of blessing in the years past, such as 1859, 1860, 1866 and 1867, 1874 and 1875; years of the right hand of the Most High.

> "Wilt Thou not revive us again?
> O Lord! revive Thy work."

"The publication of such articles cannot be otherwise than very profitable.

"May the blessing of the Lord rest in abundant measure upon them. May the coming year be one of very special blessing on all the good work in which you are engaged. May it be characterised by glorious Gospel successes.—I am, ever yours most truly,   JOHN DUKE."

Since the above was written, our dear friend Mr. Duke has passed away, to be for ever with the Lord.

A sad interest attaches to the foregoing letter, for after receiving it my dear friend Mr. Duke was laid aside for a number of weeks with serious illness, and then he was not, for God took him, to be with Himself for evermore. "The Lord gave, and the Lord hath taken away; blessed be the name of the Lord." Amen. Ah! how his unwavering trust in the merits of his Saviour in these days supported him, and his confidence as a covenant-keeping God, with Whom, as he himself expressed it, "the matter was settled long ago." His patience and gentleness in the midst of extreme weakness was very manifest to the sorrowing friends around, who were assured of the abundant entrance reserved for the dear sufferer, and, as it was said, "he would come forth as gold out of the furnace of trial."

A lady in Longforgan returns one of these sketches, and writes—"I remember Mr. M'Cheyne quite well, and also Tom Brown who kept the meetings in a house in the Hawkhill. He was a distant relation of my mother's. I think he went to the sea, and we lost sight of him.—I am, yours truly,

Mrs. H. P."

II

THERE were gracious and even marvellous doings of the Lord by His much-honoured servant, the Rev. Murray M'Cheyne, of St. Peter's Church, Dundee. He was ordained in that church in November 1836. Even at this evening trial sermon, when he preached as a candidate on 14th August preceding, the blessing of God fell upon two souls as he discoursed from the book of Ruth. One might think how unlikely a part of Scripture that was to expect it to be blessed. Ah! one word of God can do it when the preacher is a God-sent man, filled with the Spirit, as the sacred poet writes :—

> "One word from Thee dispels our fears,
> And gilds the gloom of night."

And another precious sentence might be quoted which has often been very helpful to me :—" Heaviness in the heart of man maketh it stoop, but a good word maketh it glad" (Prov. xii. 25). At that time Mr. M'Cheyne had a congregation of 1100 hearers, and when he was introduced to them souls were awakened by his first sermon, as he afterwards learned. In his interesting diary, which was partly published after his death, it was observed that he had entered in it on that day :—" Felt given over

to God, as one bought with a price," which was a
fit and solemn testimony of the feelings of this
holy man of God. He tried to be right with God,
he tried to please God. It was said of him by a
servant girl, in a house where he stayed, "He's
deein' to hae folk converted." He seemed to have a
favourite Psalm tune, named Newington, which is a very
sweet and lovely one, and if you will sing it devotion-
ally, when you have time, or at your family worship,
to the words in Psalm lxxxix. 15-18, in memory of
dear Mr. M'Cheyne, it may be a blessed exercise to your
soul :—

> "O greatly bless'd the people are
> The joyful sound that know ;
> In brightness of Thy face, O Lord,
> They ever on shall go.
>
> "They in Thy name shall all the day
> Rejoice exceedingly ;
> And in Thy righteousness shall they
> Exalted be on high.
>
> "Because the glory of their strength
> Doth only stand in Thee ;
> And in Thy favour shall our horn
> And power exalted be.
>
> "For God is our defence, and He
> To us doth safety bring :
> The Holy One of Israel
> Is our Almighty King."

The one theme—souls to Christ—was his cry. And
when he was far from home, on his way to Palestine,
the sight of a row of poor wretched Egyptians, who
had gathered round in a small village, made him
cry out: "Oh, that I could speak their language and

tell them of salvation." When the great revival took place in St. Peter's Church and district, when he was away that time, it was likely, if not certain, that his earnest prayers and wrestlings with God, along with the manifold labours and prayers of his young assistant, Mr. W. C. Burns, and his praying people, quickly brought the blessing down. For is it not written for our encouragement to exercise a quenchless zeal for God and His noble cause:— " They shall not labour in vain, nor bring forth for trouble, for they are the seed of the blessed of the Lord, and their offspring with them. And it shall come to pass that before they call I will answer, and while they are yet speaking I will hear" (Isa. lxv. 23, 24). So we, Christians, should "labour on, the bright reward in view," and also have much prayer and faith in God that He will help us and give us the victory. At that time I was attending a Sabbath-school in another congregation, but the heavenly fire was spreading, and a number of us boys and girls, when on our way home from the classes, proposed one day to have a meeting amongst ourselves for prayer. So, on coming to our home, we asked if we might get a room, which was granted, and our meeting was held. A young girl, one of the party, led in a prayer most beautifully, and so the blessed work commenced amongst us, when our young hearts were thrilled, and, praise the Lord, that instrument of ten strings is by grace still in tune to-day. A number of other young people joined us, and our prayer-meetings were carried on week after week. But a larger gathering was held in the neighbourhood,

where some of us would go, and on Sabbath there
was an early morning prayer-meeting in the same
place (a small schoolroom), and an orphan boy from
the Dundee Orphan Institution would take the lead
generally and speak most powerfully. A favourite
portion of Scripture, which we often read at our
meetings, was in John xiv.: " Let not your heart be
troubled : ye believe in God, believe also in Me.   In
My Father's house are many mansions : if it were not
so, I would have told you.   I go to prepare a place
for you.   And if I go and prepare a place for you, I
will come again, and receive you unto Myself, that
where I am there ye may be also."

Mr. M'Cheyne found the work of the Lord prospering on returning to his flock from the Holy Land.
Crowds were in the church to meet him.   I was
there.   He brought the matters concerning their peace
before his people now in his Sabbath services.   The
things relating to eternity were often applied to the
conscience in the power of the Spirit, so that at times
the feelings of the congregation could not be re-
strained.   We will hear Mr. M'Cheyne himself now
on the subject, as he wrote as follows :—" Often an
awful and breathless silence pervaded the assembly ;
and each hearer bent forward in the posture of rapt
attention.   Serious men covered their faces to pray
that the arrows of the King of Zion might be sent
home with power to the hearts of sinners.   Again at
such a time I have heard a half-suppressed sigh
rising from many a heart, and have seen many
bathed in tears.   At other times I have heard loud
sobbing in many parts of the church, while a deep

solemnity pervaded the whole audience. I have also in some instances heard individuals cry aloud, as if they had been pierced through with a dart.

"These solemn scenes were witnessed under the preaching of different ministers, and sometimes occurred under the most tender gospel invitation. On one occasion, for instance, when the minister was speaking tenderly on the words, 'He is altogether lovely' (Song of Solomon v. 16), almost every sentence was responded to by cries of the bitterest agony. At such times I have seen persons so overcome that they could not walk or stand alone. I have known cases in which believers have been similarly affected through the fulness of their joy. I have often known such awakenings to issue in what I believe to be real conversion. I could name many of the humblest, meekest believers who at one time cried out in the church under deep agony. I have also met with cases where the sight of souls thus pierced has been blessed by God to awaken careless sinners who had come to mock.

"I am far from believing" (Mr. M'Cheyne continues) "that these signs of alarm always issue in conversion, or that the Spirit of God does not work in a more quiet manner. Sometimes, I believe, He comes like the pouring rain, sometimes like the gentle dew. Still, I would humbly state my conviction that it is the duty of all who seek the salvation of souls, and especially the duty of ministers, to long and pray for such solemn times when the arrows shall be sharp in the heart of the King's enemies, and our slumbering congregation shall be made to cry out, 'Men and brethren, what shall we do?'" (*Memoir*, p. 499).

And oh! we boys and girls got a share of the blessing in our minds, and in our meetings, as time after time we would meet to read the Scriptures and pray together, and sing the praises of Him who died. There were not many hymns sung at our meetings, psalms and paraphrases were mostly used. My aged friend, the late Mr. A. Young, Edinburgh, had just some time previously composed his very beautiful hymn :—

> "There is a happy land,
> Far, far away."

And there was another tender and touching hymn often sung by us :—

> "Oh, that will be joyful
> When we meet to part no more."

These two were exquisitely strengthening and helpful to our young minds, and we believed them, as to our own experience, as the very Truth most pure. And I believe them yet; for conscious, sweet assurance, through the blood of the Lamb, makes a sweet pillow at night. And joy and peace in believing make us happy anywhere. The soul may at times have its buffetings, temptations, and trials during the watches as day and night pass by ; but we must flee then to the Refuge set before us in the Gospel, bringing all in humble confession to the Lord, and so get peace again :

> "Peace, perfect peace, in this dark world of sin,
> The blood of Jesus whispers peace within."

"What is classic learning to us now?" said Mr. M'Cheyne to his friend Dr. Andrew Bonar, as they were both tasting that God was good in thus reviving and quickening the souls around them. "I seem to know more of the Lord Jesus Christ than of the most intimate friend I have on earth."

I would say, however, that perhaps the instilling of temperance principles into the minds and hearts of the young people did not seem to bulk in the revival. But it is well that all parents should be signed total abstainers, fathers and mothers, and from early days train their children to scorn and hate drink and drunkenness, and be signed and firm abstainers, and labour earnestly in this noble work of God. Of course, every minister should be on the Lord's side in this good work, and I now humbly exhort the elders who are not abstainers to come at once to the help of the Lord against the mighty. How much might be done for the glory of the Lamb and for eternity by the thousands of elders in the Church of Christ! How much might be done in winning souls! How much might be done against the devil's kingdom of drink, and the horrible sins which generally accompany it, if every elder was a signed abstainer, labouring in his district with firm, loving energy against these terrible evils. Perhaps there is not a district in the whole of the churches where there are not some of the members either secretly or openly drinking themselves into their graves, and ruining their souls for ever. But it is not in his own strength that the elder must seek to do his work. He should have many a heartfelt cry to God for help. I know some of its hard work, as I was ordained an elder in April 1856, with many failings.

But Dundee was not altogether without a strong witness for the temperance cause.

William Cruikshanks was raised up to be the first preacher in this quarter against the use of spirits and fermented liquors. As early as in 1829 he succeeded in establishing the Dundee Temperance Society, which was regularly organised in 1830.

He delivered lectures in Dundee and neighbourhood to crowded audiences, consisting of all classes. He was appointed a preacher to a meeting of Wesleyan Methodists in Leeds. Then he returned to Dundee, and died in the sixty-fifth year of his age.

He is buried in the Constitution Road cemetery, where a very pretty tombstone is erected to his memory by friends, and to which I contributed.

I knew a godly, humble Scotch elder once, who was very useful in his day. Modestly visiting the sick and dying, praying with the distressed and comforting the bereaved, was a work in which he delighted. Hearing that he was ill, I called at his house, read the Scriptures, and prayed with him. It was very beautiful to see him, so happy, so calm, so assured, resting on Jesus. It was interesting to see his two daughters attending to his every want. If there is anything on earth which can be viewed as a type of the beautiful and good in a family, it is to see affectionate, dutiful daughters tending an aged and dying parent. And now his strength is gone, his eyes are getting dim, his soul is getting ready, and he just waits on his adorable Redeemer coming for him as He has promised. It is solemn to sit beside his dying bed and speak about eternity, and of our meeting again by grace through the precious blood. Now farewell, earthly friends, and all whom I hold dear. Welcome, Christ: welcome, eternity: welcome, heaven. "Let me die the death of the righteous, and may my last end be like his." "The Lord gave, and the Lord hath taken away: blessed be the name of the Lord."

III

" THERE is no piece of Christian biography,"
wrote a friend to me from Abergele, "to
which I have been more deeply indebted all my life,
than that of Dr. Bonar's *Life of M'Cheyne.* The
reading of that book has always been to me a positive
means of grace."

So the Spirit, being poured out on Mr. M'Cheyne's
church and people in 1839, they would meet together
and pray and call on God with great delight and joy
in the Lord.

At that time St. Peter's Church would be open at
10 a.m. on a Communion Sabbath, and continue with
table after table till five o'clock in the afternoon.
During one of these services Mr. M'Cheyne cried
out: "Ah, Judas, I know you, I know you; you will
betray me!" This was the means of the conversion
of an old lady, whom I visited some time ago. She
told me that she was very anxious about her soul,
and visited Mr. M'Cheyne. She knelt down in
her room, and thought the very ground would
open under her feet, and in great distress she
dealt with the Lord, when at last He graciously
sent her a message of peace to her weary, troubled
heart.

"Oh the peace that Jesus gives,
  Peace I never knew before;
And my way has brighter grown
  Since I learned to trust Him more."
                    Salvation Army Hymns.

A time of prayer was appointed on one occasion, and it was said Mr. M'Cheyne spent the whole night in prayer privately in the open air.

"What monotony there is in the ministry of many; duty presses on the heels of duty, in an endless circle.

"But it is not so when the Spirit is quickening both the pastor and his flock.

"Then there is all the variety of life.

"It was so here.

"The Lord began to work by his means almost from the first day he came.

"There was ever one and another stricken, and going apart to weep alone."—*Memoir*, pp. 67, 68.

"Is there any sad heart that is heavy laden?
  Any one here, any one here?
Is there any poor soul who would love the Saviour?
  Come and we will help you on your way.
Just as you are, the Lord will save you,
  Come without delay:
Is there any poor soul who would follow Jesus?
  Come, and we will help you on your way."
                    Revival Hymn.

In these moments or times of revival, when the blessed Holy Spirit draws near to the people of God in power and saving love, our hearts are lifted above the world, our souls pant after God, and much of our time is spent in adoring and admiring and praising the Lord Jesus who died for us on Calvary's rugged tree.

"Wilt Thou not revive us again, that Thy people may rejoice in Thee?" wrote King David of old (Ps. lxxxv. 6). And Nehemiah proclaimed a fast and repentance for his people. "And they stood up in their place and read in the book of the law of the Lord their God one-fourth part of the day, and another fourth part they confessed and worshipped the Lord their God" (Neh. ix. 3).

And we were reading some time ago the life of Elliot, the missionary to the Indians of America, where he mentions an awakening amongst them, and regulations were adopted "in the end of the eleventh month, 1647. They strictly prohibited intemperance, impurity, falsehood, gambling, and quarrels, under severe fines. They threatened the crimes of murder and adultery with death; and enjoined neatness, cleanliness, industry, the payment of debts, and the observance of the other duties of morality."

"And the Indians at Concord did not rest satisfied with consenting to observe these regulations; they appointed a respectable Englishman as a recorder to see them carried into execution, and they generally abandoned their savage habits. They established the worship of God in their families, and according to their ability they addressed themselves, morning and evening, to the Father of Mercies, who has graciously promised to hear the faithful prayers of the most humble supplicants. They observed the Sabbath, and employed some of its precious hours in repeating to one another the religious instructions which, under all their disadvantages, they had obtained."—*Life of Elliot*, pp. 63, 64.

How delightful to think that under the Holy Word of God even the savage breast can be at peace by faith in God, have meltings of heart under the felt love of Jesus, and begin to rouse up and endeavour to live for eternity. Oh, let us not be behind the poor Indian!

In our favoured land let us seek to get deep into the spiritual life, especially in its practice, to love Jesus, and to love our neighbour as ourselves.

About this time Mr. M'Cheyne was much in attendance on a dying boy named Jamie Laing, who had, it seems, a bright and happy and wonderfully intelligent experience of the love of Jesus. A narrative of the case was written by Mr. M'Cheyne some time after the boy's death, entitled *Another Lily Gathered*, which may be fairly reckoned as one of the classics of juvenile religious biography, and is very touching. Not only we young people were granted very great blessings in these happy early days, but the old folks were stirred to love and to service.

Homes may have been somewhat brightened; some would haply forsake the public-house; and gaiety might give place to sober, holy living. Now the dusty Bible had to be taken down from the shelf. Now family worship may have been commenced or resumed. Now the motto for the shop and the market must be "Honest and true." The profane oath must now be heard no more. The holy Sabbath day had now to be hallowed. Prayer was a delight, and prayer-meetings were held all along the line.

And conscience, God's light within the human breast, had spoken no doubt loudly to many of their coarse and evil and wicked habits, indulgences, and ways, saying, "Depart ye, depart ye, go ye out from thence, touch no unclean thing; go ye out of the midst of her; be ye clean that bear the vessels of the Lord" (Isa. lii. 11).

We were acquainted at this period with a good and kind and pious family, I think strict abstainers, and useful and helpful in all the neighbourhood were Mr. and Mrs. Moncur. They lived somewhat near St. Peter's Church in Dundee, and were highly respected by all around.

What an influence this has upon a community, as it is known that a *man of principle* is at hand to consult, and as the lady would often be sent for to help, in cases of sickness and distress, by rich and poor alike.

> "Thy deeds let sacred justice rule,
>   Thy heart let mercy fill,
> And, walking humbly with thy God,
>   To Him resign thy will."

Some time before the death of my friend, the late Albert Midlane, the author of "There's a home for little children, above the bright blue sky," he wrote me as follows:—

"Dear M'Cheyne! his life seems a presentiment of the 'Morning Star.' It has ever charmed me. Amongst men, almost the *sweetest* I know.

"Nothing can be better than reproducing the scenes of the past, with all their hallowed associations. One can only say, *Go forward.* Let the *light* of the past shame the indifference of the—alas!—present.

"Things in England are darkening; one can almost

say, 'Truth is fallen in the streets.' Yet our God is true. 'Bear up, dear brother, *whose steps follow.'* May He largely bless you. 'The time is at hand.' With Christian love from dear Mrs. Midlane.—Yours ever, ALBERT MIDLANE."

And the Rev. Donald Davidson of Invergowrie (to the old ruined church of which Mr. M'Cheyne used to go and meditate) wrote me more than a year ago an encouraging word :—" I thank you most heartily for giving me the privilege of perusing your precious reminiscences of R. M. M'Cheyne. The days of which your notes speak (chap. xviii.) were indeed days of the Son of Man upon the earth. Well might we pray—

> " ' O send again that heavenly hour,
>   That vision so divine.'

" I seldom pass the old Dargie Church ruins without thinking of the saintly M'Cheyne, for he used to come out to Invergowrie, and in the graveyard of the church sit and meditate and pray."

The Rev. John Lyon was also a revival helper in these days. He was minister of the church at Banton, near Kilsyth. I remember hearing him preach a solemn sermon in St. Peter's, on the text, Phil. iii. 18, 19: "For many walk, of whom I have told you often, and now tell you even weeping, that they are the enemies of the Cross of Christ: whose end is destruction, whose God is their belly, and whose glory is in their shame, who mind earthly things." Dear Mr. Lyon has long ago left us for the Better Land on high.

The Rev. John M'Neill, of Christ Church, Westminster Road, wrote me returning chapters xix. and xx.—and said, " Many thanks for the sight of the articles about M'Cheyne, and revival days. They are kindling sketches. I felt as I read them a revival glow. 'Return, O Lord: how long? Let it repent Thee concerning Thy servants.' Oh for a day—if it were only a day—of God's own power.—Yours ever, JOHN M'NEILL."

The chapter, No. 16, I took the liberty to send to a minister in the north of Scotland, who very kindly wrote returning it :—" Many thanks for your letter and article, which I have read with interest. It is curious that I have been reading for some time Bonar's *Life of Mr. M'Cheyne* with great enjoyment, and I trust spiritual profit. I join with you in praying for a revival of true religion among us. With kindest wishes."

And that very kind and busy man, Principal Alexander Whyte, D.D., Edinburgh, has received several of these chapters.

When returning No. 19, he wrote :—" DEAR MR. SMITH,—My favourite text these days is the last three verses of Micah. This great passage is inexhaustible. Warm regards.—A. WHYTE."

The following verses are referred to :—

18th verse—" Who is a God like unto Thee, that pardoneth iniquity, and passeth by the transgression of the remnant of His heritage? He retaineth not His anger for ever, because He delighteth in mercy."

19th verse—" He will turn again; He will have compassion upon us; He will subdue our iniquities;

and Thou wilt cast all their sins into the depths of the sea."

20th verse—" Thou wilt perform the truth to Jacob, and the mercy to Abraham, which Thou hast sworn unto our father, from the days of old."

Again he wrote me :—

> "' How sweet the name of Jesus sounds
>   In a believer's ear.
> It soothes his sorrows, heals his wounds,
>   And drives away his fear.'—JOHN NEWTON.

" I found it helpful yesterday, at death-beds and sick-beds.—A. W.

" Sat."

An old lady, a convert of M'Cheyne's, told me what an awful time of conviction of sin she had in these days. No one had ever spoken to her about her soul ; then a woman took her to Mr. M'Cheyne, who spoke to her, as the tears ran down her cheeks like a river.

She said, " I did not understand him, and felt as if I was lost, lost, lost—twice lost."

At night, when they were all asleep, she was praying, and a light passed three times before her eyes, which made her happy for a week.

Mr. M'Cheyne said in church, " You with the tears trickling down, ask Him now—ask Him, and He will give you the Living Water." Then she got help, that when we believed, Jesus Christ drank up our sins upon the cross.

So she then believed, and got peace ; and nothing

has disturbed it more. "And I am just lippening," she said, "on Him doing all for me."

And a titled lady, who sat under Mr. M'Cheyne when young, wrote me as follows :—

"I return you the article (No. 18) on Mr. M'Cheyne, with many thanks for giving me the perusal of it. With many drawbacks, Scotland has improved since those days of our early youth. There are many more good men in all our churches now than there were then. Even within these last few years, what an improvement in the tone of good men towards each other! It has been pleasant to read of the kindly, courteous speeches in the two great assemblies that held their sittings in Edinburgh lately. What a difference there has been there lately, even within the last few years.

"Complete unity is impossible, but kindly Christian co-operation and courtesy are at last possible. We may thank God for allowing us to see the beginning of the days in the Foreign Mission field, where our Presbyterian missionaries are uniting their institutions and cordially co-operating in their missionary stations.

"One of the results of Christian unity, according to our Lord's High Priestly prayer before His crucifixion, was to lie in this—'That the world may believe that Thou hast sent Me.' With kind regards, believe me, yours very truly."

IV

I RECEIVED a letter from a friend in Irvine as follows :—

" I have been deeply interested in your account of the work in connection with R. Murray M'Cheyne, as in the winter of 1859, sitting reading his life and letters, I got deliverance to my burdened heart. I have seen many ups and downs during these forty years, but still have a deep relish for 1 Cor. vi. 20— 'For we are bought with a price; therefore glorify God in your body, and in your spirit, which are God's."

In Robert Murray M'Cheyne we had a hymn writer as well as preacher, whose sweet and useful *Songs of Zion* are more or less still used with much acceptance in many of our best collections. How clear and true and soul-refreshing is the one, I suppose, from his own personal experience, entitled "Jehovah Tsidkenu." The watchword of the Reformers, "The Lord our Righteousness."

"I once was a stranger to grace and to God,
   I knew not my danger, and felt not my load;
   Though friends spoke in rapture of Christ on the tree,
   Jehovah Tsidkenu was nothing to me.

"I oft read with pleasure, to soothe or engage,
   Isaiah's wild measure or John's simple page,

But e'en when they pictured the blood-sprinkled tree,
Jehovah Tsidkenu seemed nothing to me.

"When free grace awoke me by light from on high,
Then legal fears shook me, I trembled to die;
No refuge, no safety, in self could I see,
Jehovah Tsidkenu my Saviour must be.

"My terrors all vanished before the sweet name,
My guilty fears banished; with boldness I came
To drink at the Fountain, life-giving and free,
Jehovah Tsidkenu is all things to me.

"Even treading the valley, the Shadow of Death,
This watchword shall rally my faltering breath,
For when from life's fever my God sets me free,
Jehovah Tsidkenu my death-song shall be."

Mr. M'Cheyne sought to encourage Sabbath-schools to be held in all the districts of his parish, and some of his sweet, simple tracts and hymns were written for these schools, and the verses, "Oil for the Lamp," was written to impress the parable of the Ten Virgins (Matt. xxv. 1-13), on a class of Sabbath-scholars in 1841 :—

"Learn here, my child, how vain
This world with all its lies;
Those who the Kingdom gain
Alone are truly wise.

"Is your lamp filled, my child,
With oil from Christ above?
Has He your heart, so wild,
Made soft and full of love?

"Then you are ready now,
With Christ to enter in,
To see His holy brow,
And bid farewell to sin."

" Reasons why children should fly to Christ" was
his first simple little tract, written in 1839, and "The
Lambs of the Flock" was another at a later period.
One evening, after visiting some of the Sabbath-
schools, he wrote:—"Had considerable joy in teaching the children. Oh, for real heart-work among
them!" He did not reckon it vain to use his talents
in order to attract their attention, for he regarded the
soul of a child as infinitely precious. " Ever watchful
for opportunities," the *Memoir* adds, "on the blank
leaf of a book which he had sent to a little boy of
his congregation, he wrote these simple lines :—

> " ' Peace be to thee, gentle boy !
> Many years of health and joy ;
> Love your Bible more than play,
> Grow in wisdom every day ;
> Like the lark on hovering wing,
> Early rise, and mount, and sing :
> Like the dove that found no rest
> Till it flew to Noah's breast ;
> Rest not in this world of sin,
> Till the Saviour take thee in.' "

I attended a district school for some time, where
the children of the neighbourhood were collected for
instruction and prayer. The teacher was an aged
man, and I liked to go to hear him. It was announced
that our minister was to visit the school. He was a
good man and very kind to children, but different in
manner and style to Mr. M'Cheyne. All that I
recollect is that he gave us a text of Scripture, that
we might learn it by heart and repeat it to him at
his next visit, as follows:—" The wicked are like
the troubled sea when it cannot rest, whose waters

cast up mire and dirt" (Isa. lvii. 20).   Mr. M'Cheyne,
when at the Edinburgh University, made music and
poetry his recreations, and the great Professor Wilson
adjudged him the prize in the class of Moral Philosophy for a poem on "The Covenanters."   Some
years ago I communicated with Dr. Andrew Bonar,
who wrote his *Memoir*, to see if this poem was still
in existence.   He referred me to Mr. M'Cheyne's
now deceased sister Eliza, but she did not seem to
know about it at all.   Mr. M'Cheyne's feelings about
the world are well expressed in one of his verses as
follows :—

> "O ! ye that fain would find the joy,
>   The only one without alloy,
>   Which never is deceiving,
>   Come to the Well of Life with me,
>   And drink as it is proffered—free ;
>   The Gospel draught receiving."

From early childhood Mr. M'Cheyne's temper was
affectionate and amiable, and his biographer mentions
that his melodious voice and powers of recitation
made him somewhat eminent in his English class.
His companions speak of him then as of a light, tall
form, noble in his disposition, disdaining everything
like meanness or deceit.

It seems to have been the death of his eldest
brother David, which was the event awakening him
from the sleep of nature, and brought the first beam
of Divine light into his soul.   He tried to paint a
portrait of David from memory, but setting the
pencil aside he wrote some beautiful lines on the
subject, these amongst the rest :—

"Oh ! how oft that eye
Would turn on me, with pity's tenderest look,
And only half upbraiding bid me flee
From the vain idols of my boyish heart."

There is a sweet little hymn of his adapted for children, so simple and suited to the young mind :—

"Like mist on the mountain,
Like ships on the sea,
So swiftly the years
Of our pilgrimage flee ;
In the grave of our fathers,
How soon we shall lie ;
Dear children, to-day
To a Saviour fly.

"Do you ask me for pleasure ?
Then lean on His breast,
For there the sin-laden
And weary find rest.
In the valley of death
You will, triumphing, cry,
'If this be called dying,
'Tis pleasant to die.'"

His verses on the death of a believing boy are very tender and touching ; a few of which I give here, and they may comfort some mourner in Zion (see *Memoir*) :—

"The Sabbath sun rose bright and clear,
When thine was setting on us here,
To shine more bright in yonder sphere,
Farewell, we'll meet again.

"I stood beside thy silent bed,
Thy marble brow was cold and dead,
Thy gentle soul was fled—was fled.
Dear boy, we'll meet again.

"Yes, parents! smile through all your tears,
A Crown of Life your darling wears.
The grave, a shady porch appears,
To where we'll meet again.

"The precious dust beneath that lies,
Shall at the call of Jesus rise
To meet the Bridegroom in the skies
That day; we'll meet again."

When Mr. M'Cheyne was in Palestine, he wrote
some verses at the foot of Mount Carmel, a verse or
two of which I give:—

" Beneath Moriah's rocky side
A gentle fountain springs;
Silent and soft its waters glide,
Like the peace the Spirit brings.
The thirsty Arab stoops to drink
Of the cool and quiet wave,
And the thirsty spirit stops to think
Of Him who came to save."

The piece written at the sea of Galilee, 16th July
1839, has always had a charm for me. The following
verses of the hymn I consider simply lovely, almost
unequalled by the best writers:—

" How pleasant to me thy deep blue wave,
O Sea of Galilee,
For the Glorious One who came to save
Hath often stood by thee.

" Fair are the lakes in the land I love,
Where pine and heather grow;
But thou hast loveliness far above
What Nature can bestow.

" It is not that the wild gazelle
   Comes down to drink thy tide,
But He that was pierced to save from hell
   Oft wandered by thy side.

" It is not that the fig-tree grows,
   And palms, in thy soft air,
But that Sharon's fair and bleeding rose
   Once spread its fragrance there.

" O Saviour ! gone to God's right hand,
   Yet the same Saviour still ;
Graved on Thy heart is this lovely strand,
   And every fragrant hill.

" O give me, Lord, by this sacred wave,
   Threefold Thy love divine,
That I may feed, till I find my grave,
   Thy flock—both Thine, and mine."

A short time ago a convert of Mr. M'Cheyne's
visited our home from Perthshire, and we had prayer
together. Dear old lady, still wonderfully hale and
healthy, and somewhat overflowing with grace for
the present, and happy memories of the past, as we
shall now hear :—

" I was nothing," she said, " until the Lord took me
up, and taught me, so that only by the grace of God
I am what I am. He loved me and brought me into
His banqueting house. It was a beautiful Sabbath
morning when I was led into a widow's garret by the
good Spirit of God, where a few women were met
for prayer on their way to Mr. M'Cheyne's kirk.
They were all on their knees, and I kneeled down

beside them.   Now that it was over, all stood up and
sang—

> " ' O may we stand before the Lamb,
>   When earth and seas are fled,
>   And hear the Judge pronounce our name,
>   With bessings on our head.'

I could only weep and cry out. My heart was
broken by the Spirit's power. The dear girls all ran
to their knees again. When I settled a little they
took me with them to church. His text was—'If
thou knewest the gift of God, thou wouldst have
asked of Him' (John iv. 10). I kept weeping all
the time. I was much helped by Christian friends
privately. Mr. John Mathewson, who was an elder
at that time in St. Peter's, did me much good. I
knew a few at that time who cared for anxious souls.
We heard a glorious gospel at that time. When he
read the Word, he told us the doctrine of it, so that
the foundation of our faith was steadfast, and I have
never troubled with new doctrines. Since then I have
always loved female meetings for prayer. At every
opportunity I have tried to get up, and gather in my
own house, or somewhere else, these meetings, which
have been a blessing to many, I believe, and to my own
soul also. I think it a good way also to speak at the
close of a meeting to souls—a little message from
the Lord, quietly, kindly spoken, breaks the heart.
I was born the second time in 1840, and now I am
eighty-two years old. As the hymn says—

> " 'I am here alive to day,
>   Bless His name, bless His Name.' "

An aged minister, the Rev. J. H. Wells, Bridge of
Earn, wrote me a good while ago, that a lady told
him she was admitted to the Communion by
M'Cheyne when she was eleven years of age. And
a member of his own church heard (when a child)
Mr. M'Cheyne preach on " The Great White Throne,"
about 1841.

The Parish Church was crowded up to the pulpit
door, and the impression made was great.

Another of his members who died at a great age
" read no books but her Bible and M'Cheyne's
Memoirs.

" That book used to be very well known and prized
in this parish. It occupies the same place of
honour in Scotland, that Henry Martyn's *Memoirs*
occupies in England. The two men resembled
each other much, and did more for Christ's cause by
their death than by their life. M'Cheyne's death
caused an extraordinary quickening of five of his
favourite friends and companions, each of whom God
permitted to live to a great age, and to do much :
Dr. Horatius Bonar, Dr. Andrew Bonar, Dr. Moody
Stuart, Mr. Alexander Cumming, Mr. Purves of
Jedburgh.

" I remember," Mr. Wells continues, " one of his
expressions, which I read years ago, ' Preach hell
tenderly,' *i.e.* with heart-breaking sorrow and compassion, out of a deep conviction of the terrible
reality of heaven and hell. One who has not those
feelings (Mr. M'Cheyne means) ought not to preach
it at all. You do well to remind readers of that great
servant of Christ. One thing more. His first

question to a young communicant usually was, Are
you saved?   Few ministers in our day dare to ask
this, although many godly ministers will in a round-
about way approach as near as possible to this."

The Rev. Henry Montgomery, Belfast, wrote me
some time ago as follows:—"Mrs. Montgomery and
I have both read the proof copy of what you are
publishing in the way of reminiscences of the old
revival times.   We have read what you have written
with great interest, and my impression is, that it is
bound to produce good results; in that it tells what
the Lord has done in other days, and it should lead
to prayer and renewed effort, that we may see
'times of refreshing,' like those in the days gone
by."

And again he wrote me:—

"Let me send three F's from God's Word.

"Fret not; this is in Ps. xxxvii., regarding evil
doers.

"Faint   not;   Heb. xii., 'Consider   them   that
endured.'

"Fear not ; God's message to Abraham, ' Fear not,
I am thy shield,' etc.—Ever yours in the good hope
through grace, HENRY MONTGOMERY."

And I am just favoured by Mr. Birkmyre Scott
with a look of Mr. M'Cheyne's letter in his own
handwriting to a lady who was in deep anxiety about
her soul.

"My grandmother," Mr. Scott writes, "Mrs. Scott,
Dysart, near Montrose, was at that time (1840) in
deep anxiety. Mrs. Robertson, a minister's widow,

a mutual friend, told M'Cheyne about her. Then he
wrote the letter. After its receipt, Mrs. Robertson
invited my grandmother to visit her, and to meet
Mr. M'Cheyne, which she did. When she returned
she had come into the light. In the *Memoirs*, in
Mr. M'Cheyne's diary, or one of his letters, he says:
'At this time one came from the north to seek
Christ.' My own father, a faithful gospel minister
now in glory, was born a few years after above, and
was consecrated to God before his birth. His mother
was the lady to whom the letter was written. I
trust your book will be a blessing to many.—Yours
very truly, A. B. BIRKMYRE SCOTT."

Mr. M'Cheyne's letter is a very long one, and I
would have wished if it could have been lithographed.
I give the closing sentences, in the hope that the
Holy Spirit may bless it to the reader, as follows:—

"I must not weary you. One word more. Look
at Rev. xxii. 17. Sweet, sweet words. 'Whosoever
will, let him take of the water of Life freely.' The
last invitation in the Bible, and the freest, Christ's
parting word to a world of sinners. Any one that
pleases may take this glorious way of salvation.
Can you refuse it? I am sure you cannot. Dear
friend! be persuaded by a fellow-worm not to put off
another moment. 'Behold the Lamb of God; that
taketh away the sins of the world.'

"You are sitting, like Hagar, within reach of the
well! May the Lord open your eyes and show you
all that is in Christ. I pray for you, that you may

spiritually see Jesus, and be glad that you may go to Him and find rest.

"Farewell.—Yours ever in the Lord,

"R. M. M'C.

"*20th March* 1840."

V.

WHEN the man of God is filled with the Spirit, and in humility and godly sincerity is holding himself in readiness to help the noble cause of his Redeemer, sometimes a few words spoken to a person are fruitful and blest.

One day, as Mr. M'Cheyne passed along the street, he laid his hand upon the head of a child, who, at the kind touch, looked up into the calm, solemn countenance of the minister.

"Walter," said Mr. M'Cheyne, "do you love your soul?"

Without another word he passed on. The little fellow wondered much at the strange question. The word spoken became a thought, the thought became, through grace, a living germ, and he became the devoted Rev. Walter Davidson, of Knox Free Church, Perth.—From *Revival and Revival Work*, by Rev. John Macpherson.

On one occasion Mr. M'Cheyne wrote to a little boy a kind letter, for he did not think that his time was wasted when he helped the children.

"Pray," he wrote, "that the Holy Spirit would not only make you a believing and holy lad, but make you wise in your studies also. A ray of Divine light in the soul sometimes clears up a mathematical

problem wonderfully! The smile of God calms the
spirit, and the left hand of Jesus holds up the fainting
head, and the Holy Spirit quickens the affections so
that even natural studies go on a million times more
easily and comfortably."—*Memoir*.

The above letter might be read to the young folks
in many homes these days.

One of my friends in London, Mr. W. J. Lockie,
wrote me some time ago that the notices which I
had given about the revivals in early days had been
most sweet and precious reading.

"One of my cousins," he adds, "attributes his
conversion, under God, to the perusal of *The Life of
M'Cheyne*. O for more of such men of God,
evidently led by the Spirit! We must pray to the
Lord of the harvest to raise up and thrust forth more
men, like-minded, into the field."

The above is from a real man of God himself, and
he took me at one time to the International Exhibition
in Paris, where we engaged in tract distribution, after
we had a time of prayer, as we were liable to be
apprehended by the authorities, for, alas! in Roman
Catholic countries the circulation of the Word of
God is sometimes prohibited under penalties.

And from Brechin a friend wrote to me as
follows:—"I was very pleased to read your article
on M'Cheyne's career in Dundee. It brought to my
mind many sweet remembrances of him. I used to
hear him when I was visiting my birthplace sixty
years ago, and was much pleased and greatly
refreshed. I could not stand before him at all. I
just thought, when I looked on himself, and also the

great audience, that I breathed an entirely different atmosphere than here."

After his return from his visit to the Jews in Palestine, Mr M'Cheyne dispensed the Lord's Supper to his congregation in St. Peter's Church every quarter; and his brethren in the ministry seemed to think it a privilege to be with him, to help in the good work on these occasions.

At that time the Rev. James Hamilton, then at Abernyte, afterwards in London, was invited to come and help. Mr. M'Cheyne sent him the following beautiful letter, which shows the loving nature of the intercourse which subsisted between them (see *Memoir*):—

"15th *January* 1840.

"MY DEAR FRIEND,—Will you excuse lack of ceremony and come down to-morrow and preach to us the unsearchable riches of Christ? We have the Communion on Sabbath. We have no fast day (it being quarterly communion), but only a meeting in the evening at a quarter past seven. Come, my dear sir, if you can, and refresh us with your company. Bring the fragrance of "the bundle of myrrh" (Song of Solomon i. 13) along with you, and may grace be poured into your lips.—Yours ever."

The conviction of sin which followed the preaching of the Word at such seasons may be judged of from what one of the awakened persons with whom he was conversing said to him—"I think hell would be some relief from an angry God."

In these days of the gracious work of the Holy

Spirit in the town, and feeling deep concern for the salvation of the souls under their care, a number of the ministers formed a ministerial prayer-meeting, and they met every Monday forenoon to pray together for their flocks and for their own souls!

The time of the meeting was limited to an hour and a half, in order that all who attended might form their pastoral arrangements for the day without fear of being hindered, and in addition to prayer, those present conversed on some selected topic vitally connected with their duties as ministers of Christ.

Mr. M'Cheyne was never absent from this prayer-meeting unless through absolute necessity, and the brethren scarcely remember any occasion on which some important remark did not drop from his lips. He himself reaped great profit by it. He notes:—
"*December* 8*th*. This has been a deeply interesting week. On Monday, our ministerial prayer meeting was set agoing in St. David's vestry. The hearts of all seem really in earnest in it."—*Memoir*, pp. 135, 136.

It may interest the reader to know that I have read the Word from the large Bible which was used by the ministers then, time after time, as at the Disruption it was brought to Free St. David's Church, and was often used by me as I might be conducting a prayer-meeting or Bible-class, etc., having been honoured by being the session-clerk in dear Free St. David's for many years.

I think the only texts I can remember from which I gave addresses are Ps. lxxxvi. 11–13—"Teach me Thy way, O Lord; I will walk in Thy truth: unite my heart to fear Thy name. I will praise Thee, O Lord my God, with all my heart; and I will glorify Thy name for evermore. For great is Thy mercy toward me; and Thou hast delivered my soul from the lowest hell." The next text is that delightful one in the prophet Nahum i. 7 —"The Lord is good, a stronghold in the day of trouble; and He knoweth them that trust in Him."

On the front leaves of the Bible the signatures of the ministers who attended these meetings for prayer were inscribed, but the Rev. Mr. Mackenzie, the present minister, informs me that some person has torn out these pages and carried them away. But, providentially, I many years ago took a copy of these honoured names, and now give them here in the order in which they were written; and, further, every one of these ministers, whom I knew by sight or more intimately, has as far as I know gone to his reward in glory.

"Now with triumphal palms they stand
Before the throne on high,
And serve the God they love amidst
The glories of the sky."
Paraphrase lxvi. 3.

The following is an exact list of the signatures, copied by me from the Bible many year ago, namely :—

John Roxburgh, minister of St. John's.
George Lewis, minister of St. David's.
Robt. Murray M'Cheyne, minister of St. Peter's.
James Ewing, minister of St. Andrew's.

John Baxter, minister of Hilltown.
Patrick A. Miller, minister of Maxwelltown.
James Law, chaplain to the seamen.
Alexander Macpherson, minister of Dudhope.
Alexander Fairweather, preacher of the Gospel.
John Mackail, preacher of the Gospel.
Wm. C. Burns, preacher of the Gospel.
George Ogilvy, preacher of the Gospel.
Robert Aitken, minister of Willison.
Alfred Gatherer, preacher of the Gospel.
George Brown, preacher of the Gospel.
Thomas Robinson, minister of Mariners.
Edward Cross, minister of Monifieth.
J. M'Dougall, minister of Chapelshade.
Alex. O. Laird, minister of St. John's.
Thomas Hill, minister of Willison.
John Lyon, minister of Broughty Ferry.
William Wilson, minister of Mariners.
Thomas B. Dodds, minister of Lochee.
Islay Burns, minister of St. Peter's.

Surely the labours and prayers of all these faithful
ministers now gone to their rest will bear fruit still,
in Dundee and district; and as we boys and girls
in the days of M'Cheyne had the spirit of prayer
poured out into our young hearts, let us trust that
we will see times of blessing amongst the young
over our land again, when many shall be won over
to Jesus and live for Him.

O Lord, may the day soon arrive when our young
people, and old as well, will spend their lives in the
cause of temperance and godliness, so that the

glory of God may be advanced and the noble cause
of our dear Redeemer more and more promoted
over all the lands.

> "The beam that shines from Zion Hill
>   Shall lighten every land;
> The King who reigns in Salem's towers
>   Shall all the world command."
>
> *Paraphrase* xviii. 3.

In writing a letter to Dr. Andrew Bonar, dated
2nd December 1839, by Mr. M'Cheyne, he says:—
"I have seen many of the awakened persons, and
many of the saved. Indeed, this is a pleasant place
compared to what it was. Some of the awakened
are still in the deepest anxiety and distress. They
think that coming to Christ is some strange act of
their mind, different from believing what God has
said of His Son; so much so that they will tell you
with one breath, 'I believe all that God has said,'
and yet with the next breath they complain that
they cannot come to Christ or close with Christ.
It is very hard to deal with this delusion. I find
some old people deeply shaken; they feel insecure.
One confirmed drunkard has come to me, and is, I
believe, now a saved man. Some little children are
evidently saved. One convert of eleven years old
is a singular instance of Divine grace. When I
asked if she desired to be made holy, she said—
'Indeed, I often wish I was awa' that I might sin
nae mair.' A. S., of fifteen, is a fine tender-hearted
believer. W. S., ten, is also a happy boy."—See
Memoir.

Here again we see how tender he was. He touched the heart when he wrote, or spoke, or preached. He touched the feelings—there was no cold, dry talk with Mr. M'Cheyne.

A very great point in a sermon is the heart. "My heart said unto Thee: Thy face, Lord, will I seek" (Ps. xxvii. 8).

Yes, preacher, give us always something to touch the heart, the centre of the affections, the fountain of our love, the kernel which our Saviour wants as He says: "My son, give me thine heart" (Prov. xxiii. 26).

A friend of mine, the late Dr. S., was dying, and he delighted in Mr. M'Cheyne's verses, entitled "I am a debtor." Jesus *died* for us; therefore we should love and serve Him in return.

> "When this passing world is done,
>   When has sunk yon glaring sun,
>   When we stand with Christ in glory,
>   Looking o'er life's finished story,.
>   Then, Lord, shall I fully know—
>   Not till then—how much I owe.

> "Chosen, not for good in me,
>   Wakened up from wrath to flee;
>   Hidden in the Saviour's side,
>   By the Spirit sanctified,
>   Teach me, Lord, on earth to show,
>   By my love, how much I owe."

> The poem is dated March 1837.

And in that beautiful book, *Revival and Revival Work*, by Rev. John Macpherson, Hilltown Church, Dundee, he has the following lovely passage, p. 35, in regard to our giving our heart to Jesus, believing and being saved, as it is written, "Believe on the Lord Jesus Christ, and thou shalt be saved" (Acts xvi. 31):—

"Assurance of personal salvation came more widely to be regarded as the privilege of every Christian.

"It was held by a vastly increased number that it was neither unreasonable nor unscriptural that young believers should have as real joy and peace in believing as the ripest saints.

"It is worthy of note, that the doctrine of assurance, and the singing of Gospel hymns, ever rise and fall with the Church's life. When the Church is revived, her sons, happy in the consciousness of the love of God, sing their experience in suitable songs of praise."

So, I will say, after the above encouraging words from Mr. Macpherson, O that many enquirers would come in our day, to ask and to find the way to Jesus, and be saved and happy for ever!

VI

SOMETIMES Mr. M'Cheyne was very weak in health, and had to lay his pen aside and suffer quietly, in the hope of being able to preach again. When his heart was troubling him, he would say to himself, " Farewell, blessed work of the Gospel ministry, happy days of preaching Christ and Him crucified, winning jewels for an eternal crown." And then, again, when it has abated, " I feel as if I would stand up once more to tell all the world what the Lord of Glory has done for sinners. All my ideas of peace and joy are linked in with my Bible, and I would not give the hours of secret converse with it for all the other hours I spend in this world. I would humbly suggest for the consideration of all ministers, whether we should not preach more in the manner of God's Word. Is not the Word the sword of the Spirit? Brown of Haddington," he continued, " used to preach as if he had read no other book than the Bible. It is the Truth of God in its naked simplicity, that the Spirit will most honour and bless. ' Sanctify them through Thy Truth ; Thy Word is Truth ' (John xvii. 17)."

A good, kind friend of mine told me several years ago how his mother used to take him to the early morning meetings in St. Peter's Church at eight in the morning, in these brave days of old.

He remembers Mr. M'Cheyne quite well, and many of the early scenes and incidents connected with this dear minister. He said he was one of the praying boys then, and assured me that to him there is still a halo in a way around M'Cheyne's grave. We agreed that we had to go on in childlike simplicity, loving Jesus to the end of the day.

Some years ago I asked Dr. Andrew Bonar where I could get Mr. M'Cheyne's little book, entitled *Daily Bread*. The good doctor replied as follows :—

"GLASGOW, 28*th November* 1890.

DEAR MR. SMITH,—You wish Mr. M'Cheyne's little book showing how to read the Bible through in the course of the year. It is to be found in his *Memoir*, p. 44, etc., under the heading "Daily Bread." I have no separate copy. It was originally published as a little booklet. You must get a variety of ministers to suggest texts. Each will give what he has found helpful to himself and his people.—Yours truly, dear bro.,

(Signed) ANDREW A. BONAR."

I might here give an extract from the Rev. Islay Burns' *Life of his Father*, the pastor of Kilsyth, as to the work of grace in that town about 1838, and how it spread to Dundee:—"But, blessed be God, there have been a few very marked and decided cases, instances in which the hearts of careless and even profligate and apparently abandoned sinners have been subdued under the power of the Truth, and to all appearance savingly enlightened and changed."

"A great concourse of people, including not a few genuine friends of the Lord Jesus, assembled to our

Communion.   It is thought that not fewer than from
twelve to fifteen thousand were in and about the
town of Kilsyth upon the Lord's Day ; at the tent
the number is estimated at about ten or twelve
thousand.

"This was a remarkable night of prayer, secret and
social, probably there was not an hour or watch of
the night altogether silent.   The beds were not much
occupied ; many, like the Psalmist, prevented the
dawning of the morning.   The morning bell rung
at nine o'clock, and worship began at fully twenty
minutes to ten, both in church and at the tent.   Such
godly fear has come upon the people that scarcely a
single instance of intoxication, or any approach to it,
has been observed in the whole multitude assembled,
whereas the prevalence of this and the quarrels it
engendered brought dishonour on tent-preaching and,
in fact, extinguished it.

"The movement thus begun quickly spread during
the months that followed to other places at a greater
or a less distance from the sphere of its first mani-
festation.

"At Dundee, at Perth, at Aberdeen, in the glens
and straths of Aberfeldy and Blair Athol, and far
away in the highlands of Ross-shire, the scenes of
Kilsyth were, with slightly varying circumstances,
renewed ; and many souls were quickened from the
dead, and many more baptized with new life and
power from on high."

"Many a pastoral vineyard, in which faith and
prayer had toiled for years in vain, were during those
blessed months bathed in soft refreshing dew.

"Individual souls, too, who, from far distances and from many different parishes, had found their way to some of the great centres of the north, especially at communion times, carried with them, on their return to their respective homes, the sacred impressions they had received; while many ministers, who had either taken part in the services or were present as worshippers and witnesses, returned to their own flocks to preach the old Words of Life with new unction and power.

"Thus, from the bosom of these great fires which the Divine Spirit had kindled here and there over the land, were thousands of burning sparks cast forth on every side around, and many a live coal carried away, to kindle other fires elsewhere.

"Certain it is that from the hour of these remarkable scenes at Kilsyth and Dundee becoming generally known throughout the land, the idea of Revival as the great necessity of the Church and of the age, till then but a dim tradition of bygone days, took strong possession of the minds of Christian men, and has never since lost its hold.

"From that hour it ceased to seem to them a thing incredible that God should raise the dead; nor have there ever since been wanting among them select souls who have watched and waited before the tomb of a dead Church and of a dead world, in the sure and certain hope of a mighty shaking and a glorious resurrection ere long."

The above by Rev. Islay Burns, a calm and calculating and godly man, is to be believed, and the people of God in our day should, like these men of other times, wait on the Lord, and pray and trust in Him, to see a continuance of the good and desirable work of the Holy Spirit in our midst all along the line, for the glory of God alone. I have somewhat put such thoughts in verse as following :—

> " Spread the good news, both far and near,
>   Jesus Christ came down to save ;
> The great Jehovah loves our world,
>   And for our sins His Son He gave.

> " O let us send ten thousand forth
>   To continents and isles afar,
> Tell them that Jesus shed His blood
>   That they might have a Saviour."

What is the use of living, if we are not saved and happy in the Lord and doing our best to help our neighbour up the hill?

It need not be all work, work—money, money, in church or home. I would humbly say, from a long experience, it might rather be daily renewed consecration, more retirement with God in prayer, more sweet meditation and refreshing of our souls by the Word—the Written Word and the Living Word—the Lord Jesus Christ, with the firm determination to be total abstainers to the end of the day, and have the dear Saviour for our ONLY choice.

About that time in my young days, perhaps in 1836, or more, I visited an aged man whom I knew a little, in a great land, or large house of small rooms, near our home.

When I entered he was alone, sitting in his chair, I think, and I sat down near him. By and by I asked him how he was keeping? His reply was, spoken with great solemnity—" Whether I live, I live unto the Lord, and whether I die, I die unto the Lord; whether I live, therefore, or die, I am the Lord's." I was deeply affected by this visit and those words. It was blessed to me. The young waterer was watered himself. The fragrance of my boyish visit to the old man remains to this day. Perhaps young people should be encouraged to visit the sick, the aged, and the poor. It is Christlike to do so, either by the old or by the young.

At this time many young people—boys and girls —were having prayer-meetings in Dundee from week to week, and as there were children's meetings at the same time going on at Kilsyth during the revival there, a few letters were written by some of our party to the children's meetings there.

We also visited several Sabbath morning prayer-meetings of old people, who met to pray and sing before the churches went in. An early Sabbath morning meeting was held in numbers of the districts in the parish, and greatly enjoyed, as we would hear some pious souls in prayer for blessing on the work of the day, and dear old " Martyrdom " would perhaps be used with great spirit and in pathetic tones, as we would be parting in the name of the Lord, with our hearts aglow for God, on the sweet and peaceful Sabbath morn.

In these early days we might often be singing this favourite Psalm tune of " Martyrdom " to these verses of the 57th Psalm, which are most beautifully expressive of cardiphonia, as John Newton calls it,

"the language of the heart."   For the believer who
loves Jesus has his faith and patience tried at times,
but joy and peace in believing make him happy
anywhere:

> " Be merciful to me, O God ;
>   Thy mercy unto me
> Do thou extend ; because my soul
>   Doth put her trust in Thee :
> Yea, in the shadow of Thy wings
>   My refuge I will place,
> Until these sad calamities
>   Do wholly overpass.

> "My cry I will cause to ascend
>   Unto the Lord most high ;
> To God, who doth all things for me
>   Perform most perfectly.
> From heav'n He shall send down, and me
>   From His reproach defend
> That would devour me : God his truth
>   And mercy forth shall send."

The third verse has since then often been blessed to
me by reading Flavel's *Divine Conduct, or The
Mystery of Providence*, written on this text.   This is
a most precious little book, which I have read several
times, and would advise readers to try and get it,
from which they will find much comfort and blessing.
I can lend a copy.

There was no Sabbath cars in these times to break
the gracious peace and rest of the day, and to lure
the young to make holiday and so-called pleasure
of the Lord's Day.   And Mr. M'Cheyne was vigorous
in protesting against the proposed innovation of the
railway being run on the holy Sabbath Day, and
referred to the law of the land as ratified and enacted

by the Act 1690 of the Parliament of Scotland, in the two following clauses :—

"As it is the law of nature that in general a due proportion of time be set apart for the worship of God ; so, in His Word, by a positive, moral, and perpetual commandment binding all men in all ages, He has particularly appointed one day in seven for a Sabbath to be kept holy unto Him, which from the beginning of the world to the resurrection of Christ was the last day of the week, and from the resurrection of Christ was changed into the first day of the week, which in Scripture was called the Lord's Day, and is to be continued to the end of the world as the Christian Sabbath."

"This Sabbath is then kept holy unto the Lord, when men, after a due preparing of their hearts and ordering of their common affairs beforehand, do not only observe an holy rest all the day from their own works, words, and thoughts about their worldly employments and recreations, but also are taken up the whole time in the public and private exercises of His worship and in the duties of necessity and mercy. 'If this be true, which you know it is,' Mr. M'Cheyne wrote to the advocate for the railway, 'then you stand convicted before the British public as one who proclaimed it to be the duty of the directors to break both the law of God and the law of the land.'"—See *Memoir*.

About this time I used to observe a very aged woman standing inside the railings of her house looking about at the passers by. Then she was missed, and I heard she was dead. There were no

hearses then, I think, but the mourners carried the
coffin on spokes, or "spokes," as they were called,
and the bearers would relieve each other now and
again by carrying for a few minutes and resting for
a time. I was present looking on as the people
assembled and passed away to the grave, and I
muttered to myself—" Gone to her long home." I
did not know exactly the meaning of the words, not
understanding what long home signified. Perhaps
I had heard some one mentioning these words, but
I was deeply solemnised at the sight, as I knew the
old familiar figure had passed away and was now
being carried to the grave.

One of my early companions used to come and
call me on the Sabbath mornings to invite me to go
to a meeting with him. Some years afterwards he
went abroad, and then returned to our town and
took up a public-house. Poor fellow! One day he
suddenly died in his shop, and thus ended the life
on earth of my early friend. How dreadful it is to
be connected with drink! A policeman once told
me, as we stood opposite a public-house, the customers
of which I have more than once remonstrated with
as they would be entering it, that the average life of
a publican was five years, and since then the master
of it, alas! suddenly perished. I have heard of good
Christian professors being proprietors of this place.
Well, God may make reprisals on those who will go
on in this way, and it may be said, as you are ruining
others, He may ruin you, or yours, so withdraw in
time, and do not any longer be under this censure—
" You know the right, but still the wrong pursue."

I will tell here of one of Mr. M'Cheyne's converts, Mrs. J. M., Newport, who passed from death unto life by embracing and accepting the Lord Jesus Christ to be her Saviour and her God in her young days, then humbly sought to follow on to know Him better, from faith to faith, from strength unto strength.   I knew her for many years, and we have had prayer together, with her Christian housekeeper in general joining us many times.   But a messenger arrived one day in the form of a weak and feeble frame to warn her that the time had arrived when she must cross the river.   She was, I considered, a worthy, faithful convert of her sainted pastor of St. Peter's, Dundee, but now—

> "The Angel of the Covenant
> Was come, and, faithful to His promise, stood
> Prepared to walk with her through death's dark vale."

We laid her to rest in the Western Cemetery, Dundee, on Thursday, 29th April 1897.   "The Lord gave, and the Lord hath taken away : blessed be the name of the Lord."

VII

A CIRCULAR calling a convocation of ministers was issued to meet and consider the situation after the decision of the Auchterarder Case of the Established Church of Scotland, when the patronage battle was being fought during the ten years' conflict, "against the Erastian invasion made by the recent decision of the House of Peers on the rights and liberties of the Church of Scotland."

"In prospect of a meeting (17th November 1842), with whose proceedings such momentous issues were bound up, a proposal for united prayer was drawn up by the Rev. Mr. M'Cheyne, and disseminated widely over the country. The convocation assembled for business at seven o'clock in the evening in Roxburgh Church, Edinburgh. About four hundred and fifty ministers were present, a larger number than had ever met in council in Scotland. Dr. Chalmers was invited to take the chair. The spirit of prayer which, breathing from the lips of Mr. M'Cheyne or Dr. M'Donald (of Ferintosh), conveyed a profounder sense of the Divine presence than we ever felt before or since in the most hallowed of our Christian assemblies."—*Life of Chalmers*, p. 615.

Thus was Mr. M'Cheyne selected for high offices

by his Church in these days of agitation and of crisis.
Then he could descend without grudging to visit a
dying boy, with whom he laboured most kindly and
patiently until his young charge passed away to be
safe in the arms of Jesus for ever.

These matters may not be considered of much
importance by the young people, but it may show
them how the Lord honours those who live near to
Him ; they get to the front in any crisis. It reminds
me of our old Sabbath-school story, perhaps somewhat as follows :—How when a captain of a ship was
dying while at sea, he asked the steward—"Can
you pray, Jack?" "No, sir," was the reply. "Can
any of the hands pray?" "No, sir, but the
apprentice boy can pray." "Bring him, bring him,"
said the captain. When the boy was brought in
he was asked by his dying captain, "Could you pray
for me, boy?" The dear young lad poured out his
heart to the Lord for mercy to the soul just depart-
ing ; and so the story may hopefully end with the
Saviour's own word of promise, "Ask, and it shall
he given you ; seek, and ye shall find ; knock, and
it shall be opened unto you. For every one that
asketh receiveth ; and he that seeketh findeth ; and
to him that knocketh it shall be opened" (Matt.
vii. 7, 8). A humble, unlettered ship's boy can
thus be used of God ; and He will use you also, dear
young reader, if you follow on to know Him in
loving, godly sincerity, according as I heard Dr.
Maclaren, of Manchester, advise, namely—"Hold to
the simplicity which you learned at your mother's
knee" (as to prayer and believing and loving Jesus

and His Word); "the farther you recede from that,
you go the farther wrong."

Mr. M'Cheyne was also selected out from many
ministers to be one of the deputation to inquire into
the position of the Jews in Europe and the Holy
Land. The *Narrative* of their journey to Jerusalem,
written by Mr. M'Cheyne and Mr. Bonar, is a splendid
book. I have read in it over and over again for
many years. It wonderfully confirms the prophecies
and Bible history, gives much important information
as to the position and ways of living of God's peculiar
people, and is often savoury with holy eloquence
and zeal for God. In one place I think it tells that
one day when Mr. M'Cheyne was sitting at the edge
of a lonely wood, two men came and attacked
Mr. M'Cheyne, when a desperate struggle ensued
for about a quarter of an hour. The men then
suddenly plunged into the wood. Thus is God "in
straits a present aid."

> " God is our refuge and our strength,
>   In straits a present aid ;
> Therefore, although the earth remove,
>   We will not be afraid.
>
> " Though hills amidst the seas be cast ;
>   Though waters roaring make,
> And troubled be ; yea, though the hills
>   By swelling seas do shake :
>
> " God in the midst of her doth dwell ;
>   Nothing shall her remove :
> The Lord to her an helper will,
>   And that right early prove."
>
> *Psalm* xlvi.

This *Narrative of a Mission to the Jews* is

offered frequently in old book catalogues, and will well repay a careful and prayerful perusal. It was a great time when Mr. M'Cheyne returned to his waiting people in St. Peter's Church, Dundee, after his travels in the East, which in these early days was comparatively a great journey.

There was a large outhouse in a street near St. Peter's Church, which the neighbours utilised as a Prayer House. Numbers of the friends of Jesus would meet and sing and pray there, especially on Sabbath morning.

I remember an expression which we often used in our prayers, namely, "Forgive all our wandering thoughts and scattered imaginations"; and we also often quoted the text in Matt. xi. 28: "Come unto Me, all ye that *are weary*" (we said) "and heavy laden, and I will give you rest."

It was beautiful, as I suppose every one in the meeting could take some part, either breaking in with a simple, earnest prayer, or if called on would join in the worship with childlike (not childish) simplicity and godly sincerity, and this favourite passage of Scripture was read or recited in prayer—oh, how often!—"Let not your heart be troubled: ye believe in God, believe also in Me. In my Father's house are many mansions; if it were not so, I would have told you. I go to prepare a place for you. And if I go and prepare a place for you, I will come again, and receive you unto Myself; that where I am, there ye may be also" (John xiv. 1-3). Oh, I am glad that "the Word of the Lord endureth for ever" (1 Pet. i. 25).

It entirely suits children like we were in these days; we loved the Bible, and we believed it from board to board.

It suits young men and women, who greatly need direction in the ensnaring quicksands of life.

It suits the feeble and the frail, who are tottering along, as age has grey'd their locks; and there at the last, as they are just getting ready for eternity and the grave, in majestic heaven-born power, it points the eye of faith upwards, and says with the voice of God our Saviour: "Look unto Me, and be ye saved, all ye ends of the earth; for I am God, and there is none else" (Isa. xlv. 22).

> " O may the grave become to me
>   The bed of peaceful rest,
>   Whence I shall gladly rise at length
>   And mingle with the blest.
>
> " Cheer'd by this hope, with patient mind
>   I'll wait Heaven's high decree,
>   Till the appointed period comes ·
>   When death shall set me free."
>
> *Paraphrase* viii. 13, 14.

The revival under Mr. M'Cheyne and others in these days was very much amongst the young and the children, and I may class myself amongst the latter; and it seemed to be natural for us and delightful to go here and there to the meetings, to sing and pray and read the Bible.

And the dear old 54th Paraphrase was well known to our set, as we read it, or sung it, I daresay as a sort of testimony of our young faith and of our love

to Jesus, because there were parties who stood aloof
from us and our revival ways.

Let us seek and pray for *a revival among the young*
ere yet the heart has felt the strain the world can
on it lay; before repentance for worldliness, intemperance, or vice demands a first place in the
work. Might they not be invited early to the
Communion table to avow their love to Jesus, and
their desire henceforth to be the followers of the
Lamb?

And should not the " fruit of the vine " (Mark xiv.
24) alone be there? Should dear, young, godly,
abstaining children be forced to handle and taste
what drunkards delight in? I remember, many
years ago, that the late Mr. William Scott, Dundee,
a true man of God, invited me to go with him to
see about a very gracious and blessed revival amongst
the young in the parish of Cluny, Perthshire.

It commenced with a young boy who was
observed to be weeping, and he told that he was
weeping because of his sins—the Holy Spirit made
sin a heavy burden to him. Just as John Bunyan
speaks about Christian, " I looked and saw him open
the book and read therein, and not being able to
contain, he broke out with a-lamentable cry, saying,
'What shall I do?'" Then a second and a third
boy were brought to see themselves guilty before a
sin-hating God. At this time they began to meet
together to pray.

One day a person heard a sound of voices in a
wood near the children's schoolhouse. He approached
and listened, and found it to be two young boys

lying on the ground praying. Jesus says, "I love them that love Me, and those that seek Me early shall find Me" (Prov. viii. 17).

The girls now began to be affected, and one of them was greatly distressed about her soul. Some of them met together for prayer, and would also pray aloud when friends were beside them. Some of the wildest boys were now rejoicing in Christ as their Saviour, and had peace in believing. *There had been evangelistic meetings every night for five weeks before this work amongst the children commenced.* Perhaps it had not been expected that they would come to Jesus. What a mistake! Jesus dearly loves the young, and says, "Suffer the little children to come unto Me, and forbid them not, for of such is the Kingdom of God" (Mark x. 14).

See to it, Christian reader, that you encourage your young people at home to give their hearts to Jesus now. Place no obstacles in their way — "Forbid them not." One night it was asked that all those who were happy in the Lord should meet together. About thirty assembled.

They were asked one by one if they were happy in the Lord, and each answered yes. The effect was very blessed, and one who was present fell on his knees and blessed the Lord aloud for His gracious work amongst the dear children and His day of power. I met with and addressed some of these lambs of the flock that day Mr. Scott and I were amongst them; it was a time of joy and rejoicing to our hearts. Now they are scattered, and some may have gone home to glory. Oh, let us care for our

children's souls, and all seek to live so as to love and
serve the dear Saviour, who lovingly says :—

"O children, hither do ye come,
And unto Me give ear :
I shall you teach to understand
How ye the Lord should fear."
Psalm xxxiv. 11.

Mr. M'Cheyne in his early days had some thoughts
of being a foreign missionary.   Some days after
communion season he wrote in his diary:—" *May*
10*th*. Thought with more comfort than usual of
being a witness for Jesus in a foreign land. *June*
4*th*. Speaking with A. Somerville, by Craigleith,
conversing on missions.   If I am to go to the heathen
to speak of the unsearchable riches of Christ, this
one thing must be given me, to be out of the reach
of the baneful influence of esteem or contempt.   If
worldly motives go with me, I shall never convert
a soul, and shall lose my own in the labour."   But
though not going to the heathen as an ordained
missionary, the Lord chose him to do good work in
the foreign field, as far as Jerusalem, which interesting record remains, as we have seen, to this day
amongst us.   He wrote to a young boy at one time
who had just left his father's roof, and for whose soul
he felt much anxiety.

Ever watchful for souls, he seized this opportunity
of laying before him more fully the things belonging
to his peace.   I give a few sentences from his
Memoir :—

"Would the forgiveness of sins not make you more
happy than you are?

"However, if the Lord deal graciously with you, and touch your young heart, as I pray He may, with a desire to be forgiven and to be made a child of God, perhaps you will not take ill what I have written to you in much haste.

"Turn the Bible into prayer. Thus, if you were reading the 1st Psalm, spread the Bible on the chair before you, and kneel and pray: 'O Lord, give me the blessedness of the man,' etc.; 'Let me not stand in the counsel of the ungodly,' etc.

"This is the best way of knowing the meaning of the Bible and of learning to pray. At prayer, confess your sins by name, going over those of the past day one by one. Pray for your friends by name, father, mother, etc., etc. If you love them, surely you will pray for their souls. I know that there are prayers constantly ascending for you from your own house, and will you not pray for them back again? Do this regularly. If you pray sincerely for others, it will make you pray for yourself."

Mr. M'Cheyne was thus gently leading this young boy to the source of pardon and joy and peace. I will tell now of a little girl whom I only saw a few times at the first of her illness, but a record remains of her simple faith in the Lord Jesus Christ, her Saviour. Her father looked in to see her one day, and she cried out: "O father, you have often prayed for me that my eyes might be opened to see Truth. Now I see it—my eyes were opened last night about twelve o'clock; and I am so happy, for I am going home to be with Jesus. Do not weep for me, father,

I am only going home, and I will meet you at the
gates of heaven." She got her three younger
brothers to her bedside, and said : " Christ is waiting
for you, and if you accept Him we will all meet in
heaven. Will you therefore promise to meet me?"
Through their tears they all gave her this promise.
Then she shook hands with them, and said
" Good-bye."

"During that ever-memorable night," wrote her
father to me, "her last night on earth, while we gazed
at such a lovely picture of Christian resignation thus
manifest in the little child, it often moved us to tears,
while she was the only one who remained unmoved.
Her departure seemed to give her no more anxiety
than going from home for a few hours. Often did
she tell her sister that no one would sit at her
bedside and remain ignorant of her precious peace,
which seemed to flow in her heart like a deep river
without a ripple.

" As the morning bells were ringing her spirit fled.
Heaven then received another saint within its portals,
and she joined that blessed One who, while He
tabernacled here below, was numbered with trans-
gressors; so now with Him she is numbered unto
Life Eternal."

O my dear reader ! See to it that you are labouring to get all your children saved.

Just while I have been arranging these chapters,
some quite young people have been writing me that
they have given their hearts to Jesus.

"Whose faith follow," and let us all be happy in
the Lord, and live for Him.

Mr. J. B. Gillies, of Edinburgh, returned Sketch xv., saying :—" Let us feel assured and act on the conviction that the Lord's hand is not shortened, that it can work mighty as in the past.

"There is no promise in Scripture more plain and direct than that our Father in heaven will give the Holy Spirit for the asking."

Praise God! let us take courage, and pray on.

God hears prayer!

The Rev. Mr. Bisset, of Fyvie, sends me a good word :—" It is refreshing indeed to go back to these days when the Gospel had its true work in the hearts of men. I am persuaded we ought to look for the same results to-day, but we must also look for the same power that produced these results. Manifestly in the Gospel we ought to place clear issues before men.— Yours very sincerely, JOHN H. J. BISSET."

My old esteemed friend, Rev. Henry W. Bell, Aberdeen, who was for some years a minister in Dundee, and a valiant open-air speaker, writes me the following letter when returning four of my sketches, Nos. 1, 6, 16, 21 :—

"I have read them with great interest and profit.

"The special value of your articles lies in the fact that they are by one who personally knew that holy man of God, and saw the great work which God wrought through him, and who also knew many who had known him and his labours, and had been blessed through them."

"When I went to Dundee in 1864 to assist Rev. Wm. Arnot Stirling, of Chalmers' Free Church, and

afterwards, on his death, became his successor, I
found everywhere the fragrance of the memory of
M'Cheyne. What a ministry that must have been
which, short as it was, left such a savour and influence behind! I dare say people wonder why
that ministry was so short. It seems to me that
M'Cheyne was so ripe for heaven that God wished
him in the heavenly glory, and so called him into
it. Then his work, though short, *was done*; and
his early death was to do far more than his life could
have done, if it had been protracted for many years.
Like Samson, but in a spiritual sense, God's servant
slew more in his death than he slew in his life
(Judg. xvi. 30). For he lives, and will ever live, in
his *Memoir and Remains* by Dr. Andrew Bonar; and
his ministry still goes on, and will never cease while
that book lives. Then it strikes me that his
influence lives and grows in those who were blessed
under him, and who are still living, like yourself and
some others; and their influence will continue
through those blessed by them, when they themselves
have gone to their reward.

"Who can measure the influence of a single
consecrated man?

"He, under God, blesses others, and so the
blessing goes on through generations."

"I remember the godly Rev. Joseph Wilson of
Abernyte telling me that M'Cheyne was once
walking along a country road, when the ground was
covered with deep and beautiful snow. A man
was seen by him walking from the opposite direction.
When they met, M'Cheyne stopped him, with a

salutation, and then said to him, "Do you know what is whiter than snow?" The man replied, "No, I do not, for snow is the whitest thing in nature." "Yes," said M'Cheyne, "there is *one* thing that is whiter." "What is it?" the man asked. M'Cheyne replied, "It is the soul that is washed in the blood of Christ" (Ps. li. 7).

VIII

THE story of the first sight of Jerusalem by Mr. M'Cheyne and the Scottish ministers of the deputation to the lost sheep of the house of Israel is very interesting, because Mr. M'Cheyne was the first of them to see it ; and he was also the first of them to enter the heavenly Jerusalem.

So I will give some extracts about it, as the young folks may not know about him, and the old may have forgotten :—

"*June 7*, 1839. This day was to be among the most eventful of our lives, as on it we hoped to reach Jerusalem. We therefore rose very early, and were mounted by four o'clock.

"The morning had not yet dawned, but the moon poured its silvery light up the valley, and enabled our guides to find the track. Even at this early hour the birds had begun their song. We now entered into what is generally believed to be the Valley of Elah. A small village lay below us in the bottom of the hollow. The voice of the turtle saluted us from its olive trees. We now ascended a much barer mountain, and by a path the steepest we had yet climbed ; yet the camels went up wonderfully. Arrived at the summit, it appeared as if we had left all cultivation behind. A bare desert of

sunburnt rocks stretches to the right, as far as the
eye can reach. We remembered the description
given by travellers of these mountains, and knew
that we were near the Holy City. Every moment
we expected to see Jerusalem. Though wearied by
our long ride, which had now lasted seven hours, we
eagerly pressed on.

"Mr. M'Cheyne, dismounting from his camel,
hurried forward on foot over the rocky pathway, till
he gained the point where the City of the Lord
comes first in sight.

"Soon all of us were on the spot—silent, buried
in thought, and wistfully gazing on the wondrous
scene where the Redeemer died.

"The distant mountains beyond the city seemed
so near that at first we mistook them for the
mountains that enclose 'the Valley of Vision,'
though they proved to be the mountains of Moab,
on the east side of the Dead Sea. As our camels
slowly approached the city, its sombre walls rose
before us; but the nearer we came to the city, the
more we felt it a solemn thing to be where 'God
manifest in the flesh' had walked.

"The feelings of that hour could not even be
spoken. We all moved forward in silence, or inter-
changing feelings only by a word.

"But we were soon to learn that all the elements
of Jerusalem's glory and beauty are still remaining
in its wonderful situation, fitting it to be once again
in the latter day, "the City of the Great King."
Worn out with incessant travelling, we were thankful
to retire, that we might refresh our weary frames and

compose our minds, which were not a little bewildered by the multitude of feelings that had passed through them this day.

"It was with feelings that can be better imagined than described that for the first time in our lives, within the gates of Jerusalem, we committed ourselves, and those dear to us—our Church, and the blessed cause in which she had sent us forth—to the care of Him who sits as a King upon the holy hill of Zion."

"We are not aware," the narrative continues, "that any clergyman of the Church of Scotland was ever privileged to visit the Holy City before, and now that four of us had been brought thus far by the good hand of our God upon us, we trusted that it might be a token for good, and perhaps the dawn of a brighter day on our beloved Church, a day of generous, self-denied exertion in behalf of scattered Israel and a perishing world."—See *Narrative*.

Mr. M'Cheyne and the Scotch deputation to Palestine arrived home, *via* Hamburg, about the middle of November 1839, when solemn thanksgiving was offered by the committee of the Church for their safe return, as they had left Dover on the morning of 12th April, having thus been about seven months absent from their congregations and their homes.

It is most interesting to read what Mr. M'Cheyne heard had been going on amongst his flock during his absence. "He listened with deepest interest to the accounts given of what had taken place in Dundee during the month of August, when he lay at the

gates of death at Bonja. The Lord had indeed
fulfilled his hopes, and answered his prayers."

The *Memoir* continues, p. 120:—

"His assistant, Mr. Burns, had been honoured of
God to open the floodgates at Dundee as well as at
Kilsyth. For some time before Mr. Burns had seen
symptoms of deeper attention than usual, and of real
anxiety in some that had hitherto been careless.
But it was after his return from Kilsyth that the
people began to melt before the Lord."

On Thursday, the second day after his return from
Kilsyth, at the close of the usual evening prayer-
meeting in St. Peter's, and when the minds of many
were deeply solemnised by the tidings which had
reached them (about the revival there), he spoke a
few words about what had for some days detained
him from them, and invited those to remain who
felt the need of an outpouring of the Spirit to convert them.

About a hundred remained, and at the conclusion
of a solemn address to these anxious souls, suddenly
the power of God seemed to descend, and all were
bathed in tears.

At a similar meeting next evening in the church,
there was much melting of heart, and intense desire
after the Beloved of the Father; and on adjourning
to the vestry, the arm of the Lord was revealed.

No sooner was the vestry door opened to admit
those who might feel anxious to converse, than a vast
number pressed in with awful eagerness.

It was like a pent-up flood breaking forth, tears
were streaming from the eyes of many, and some

fell on the ground groaning and weeping, and crying for mercy.

Onward from that evening meetings were held every day for many weeks, and the extraordinary nature of the work justified and called for extra-ordinary services.

The whole town was moved.

Many believers doubted; the ungodly raged; but the Word of God grew mightily and prevailed.

Instances occurred where whole families were affected at once, and each could be found mourning apart, affording a specimen of the times spoken of by Zech. xii. 12: "And the land shall mourn, every family apart," etc.

The Rev. John Baxter of Hilltown, Dundee, the Rev. James Hamilton of Abernyte, afterwards of London, and other men of God in the vicinity, hastened to aid in the work. The Rev. John Roxburgh of St. John's, and the Rev. George Lewis of St. David's examined the work impartially and judiciously, and testified it to be of God.

Dr. M'Donald of Ferintosh, a man of God, well experienced in revivals, came to the spot and put to his seal also, and continued in town preaching in St. David's Church to the anxious multitudes during ten days.

How many of those who were thus awfully awakened were really brought to the truth it was impossible to ascertain. When Mr. M'Cheyne arrived, drop after drop was still dropping from the clouds. —*Memoir*, p. 121.

I cannot refrain from giving another bit as to his

first appearance in St. Peter's Church, for I was there.
"His people, who had never ceased to pray for him,
welcomed his arrival amongst them with the greatest
joy. He reached Dundee on a Thursday afternoon,
and in the evening of the same day, being the usual
time for prayer in St. Peter's, after a short meditation,
he hastened to the church, there to render thanks to
the Lord, and to speak once more to his flock. The
appearance of the church that evening, and the aspect
of the people, he never could forget. Many of his
brethren were present to welcome him, and to hear
the first words of his opened lips. There was not a
seat in the church unoccupied; the passages were
completely filled, and the stairs up to the pulpit
were crowded, on the one side with the aged, on the
other with eagerly listening children.

Many a face was seen gazing on their restored
pastor, many were weeping under the unhealed
wounds of conviction, all were still and calm, in-
tensely earnest to hear. He gave out Psalm lxvi., and
the manner of singing, which had been remarked
since the revival began, appeared to him peculiarly
sweet—"so tender and affecting, as if the people felt
that they were praising a present God."

> " All lands to God in joyful sounds
>   Aloud your voices raise ;
>   Sing forth the honour of His name,
>   And glorious make His praise."

After solemn prayer with them, he was able to
preach for above an hour.

Not knowing how long he might be permitted to

proclaim the glad tidings, he seized that opportunity not to tell of his journeyings, but to show the Way of Life to sinners.   His subject was 1 Cor. ii. 1-4 : " For I determined not to know anything among you save Jesus Christ, and Him crucified," etc.   It was a night to be remembered.

" On coming out of the church, he found the road to his house crowded with old and young, who were waiting to welcome him back.   He had to shake hands with many of them at the same time, and before this happy multitude would disperse, had to speak some words of life to them again, and pray with them where they stood."—*Memoir*, p. 22.

Mr. M'Cheyne was not strong, and his first months of labour were trying.   Much of his time was spent in visiting the sick and dying.

On 20th February 1837, he was in attendance at the funeral of a young woman, and writes :—" Prayed at her funeral.   Saw her laid in St. Peter's Church-yard, *the first laid there*, by her own desire, in the fresh mould, where never man was laid.   May it be a token that she is with Him who was laid in a new tomb."

The revival took hold of some of the inmates of a public-house ; and I think I was at several prayer-meetings there.   Of course, in these times there was little or no outcry against the drink fiend like there is nowadays, but the revival no doubt did good in that direction, amongst converts and families who had been awakened and quickened.

And a Temperance Society may have been started about that time in town ; for it is like ages since we

used to go sometimes on a Saturday night to a social
meeting in the Caledonian Hall, Castle Street, when
speeches, songs, and instrumental music made up the
temperance programme.

There were three notorious drunkards living in our
neighbourhood, and we young folks, I suppose, would
look with awful thoughts at them. Screams would
sometimes be heard coming from the wretched home
of one of them. What became of the three I do
not know, or recollect. I hope they were converted,
dear souls. It is sad to think that if they im-
penitently continued in such ways to the last, then,
alas! the warning comes to all who are like them :

> Ere night that gate may close and seal thy doom,
> Then the last low, long cry, "No room, no room,
> No room, no room !" O woeful cry, "No room !"
>
> DR. H. BONAR.

But mere temperance is not enough to rest our
souls upon. I was having prayer at one time with
Dr. Alexander Wallace, D.D., of Glasgow, and
he said (naming a friend), "O Lord, there is no
doubt he is a Good Templar ; but ah, Lord, *that is
not enough.*"

Now, though dead, may the dear doctor speak to
us all : "Temperance is not enough."

I would like to tell of one of Mr. M'Cheyne's elders,
whom I knew well for a number of years, the late
Mr. John Matthewson, Newport-on-Tay.

Since my early days I had known his figure as
he walked along the street in Dundee, near St. Peter's
Church, and in later years it was interesting to hear

him relating incidents connected with the ministry of his sainted pastor, and their joint labours at death-beds and with souls. After a long and honourable business career, he might have retired as many do, simply to enjoy their gains and live in pleasure, but he seemed more and more to devote his declining years to the Lord's work, in helping it along in word and deed. For some time he and I carried on a private Rescue Work, and had many prayers together for the salvation of the lost in our town.

His usual practice for a number of years was to rise about four in the morning for reading of Scripture and prayer, and he had at one time perhaps about thirty persons on his list, for whom he prayed.

I suppose my name had been on it, as sometimes he would give me a familiar touch and say, "There's no' a day but I mind you."

He also set apart about two hours each afternoon, between two and four o'clock, for a time of devotion and Bible reading.

His well-thumbed Bible was a sight to see, hundreds of marks in it, and some of the pages nearly dim with use and marking. At the 51st Psalm it was as if he had read it many hundreds of times. At the 14th of John it was well used, and also at some of the Epistles, and I have heard that he had stated that he had read the latter chapters of Hosea hundreds of times. The edges of the leaves of the whole Bible which he used so well in "searching the Scriptures" were much worn.

His knowledge of the Bible was so extensive and

exact that he seldom referred to a passage of Scripture without mentioning chapter and verse, and he also knew the contents of chapters by the opening verse of it.

He believed greatly in the power and willingness of the Spirit to reveal Christ to us, and he very often spoke of his belief in the power of the Holy Ghost being needed in the sinner's conversion, daily walk, and complete sanctification.

For some time he had been in failing health. One day he told me with great joy that he had the previous night the most glorious view of Christ he had ever experienced. "Oh, we are great sinners," he said, "but look at *His merits*," and he seemed filled with joy.

The holy Sabbath morning dawned, 23rd September 1877, and found him in great weakness, but peaceful and happy. His kind medical attendant, Dr. Stewart, Newport, observed a change about four o'clock in the afternoon, and said to him, "You will soon get the palm of victory." "I have got it already," was his reply, and during the day he waved his hand, pointing upwards, and said, "It's all right up there; I have a fine home to go to."

I called to see him about 5 p.m. He was lying peacefully on his bed and knew me. I took his hand, saying, "Come, Lord Jesus, come quickly," to which he responded, and he pressed my hand as I repeated to him some of the precious words of God.

He then requested us, as several of his dear ones stood around, to sing "The Lord's my Shepherd,"

and, after a short prayer, through the precious blood,
we sang " Rock of Ages," in which he joined.

After a few minutes we proceeded to sing—

> " For ever with the Lord,
>   Amen so let it be :
> Life from the dead is in that word,
>   'Tis immortality.
> Here in the body pent,
>   Absent from Him I roam ;
> Yet nightly pitch my moving tent
>   A day's march nearer home."

Just then, while we were singing, he gave a sigh,
and without the slightest struggle passed away from
the Sabbath on earth to the eternal Sabbath in glory,
to be for ever with the Lord.

Dr. Stewart came in just then, and as we stood
around we asked if our dear friend was gone.
"Yes," he replied, "he is dead, and liveth for evermore."   Then as we all stood there, observing the
solemn yet joyful scene, we sang—

> " The saints of God from death set free
>   With joy shall mount on high ;
> The heavenly hosts, with praises loud,
>   Shall meet them in the sky.
> O may we stand before the Lamb,
>   When earth and seas are fled,
> And hear the Judge pronounce our name,
>   With blessings on our head."
>
> *Paraphrase* liii. 67.

I afterwards laid my hand on his head, and prayed
that his mantle might fall on us who were left—his
mantle of prayer ; of believing the Bible ; of loving

Jesus; and having a kind heart to all. Then in due time we laid him in the grave; singing over him again, "For ever with the Lord," and thus now we have left him in his sleep of peaceful rest till the Resurrection Morn.

IX

AFTER Mr. M'Cheyne returned from Palestine, he met with the Commission of the General Assembly in the Tolbooth Church, Edinburgh.

"The attendance of members was numerous, and the proceedings were of a highly important and interesting character.

"Mr. Candlish, as convener of the Committee on the Conversion of the Jews, announced the arrival of Messrs. Bonar and M'Cheyne, two of the members of the deputation sent to make enquiries with regard to the Jews.

"The Commission agreed to hear the deputation in the evening."—*Proceedings*, 20th Nov. 1839.

At the evening sederunt, Mr. M'Cheyne rose and said :—

"We have to lament, fathers and brethren, that the senior members of the deputation have been detained by sickness at so great a distance from their native country, and till they arrive it would be obviously improper that we should lay a report on the table."

He then addressed the meeting, and gave a long *resumé* of their journey.

They considered the line of route pointed out to them very judicious.

They did not pass through Russian Poland, as

intended, because the Russian Ambassador at Constantinople refused to sign their passports because they were ecclesiastics.

They got a converted Jew, Mr. Calmoni, who was well acquainted with the languages, to accompany them to Tyre and Sidon and the other cities.

They met with many dangers and difficulties. The plague broke out in Egypt on the day of their arrival there.

When they came to Gaza the plague was there, and when they got to Jerusalem they found the plague there also, and during ten days' stay in that city five persons on an average died every day of that dreadful distemper. Most of them were poor Jews, living in great wretchedness.

Several other dangers were escaped. "We felt that we were not travelling for our own pleasure, and that our Lord was with us, and we believe that He will present us to His heavenly kingdom."

They were greatly obstructed by the Roman Catholics. "If you give a tract or a Bible to a Roman Catholic, he carries it to the priest, who carries it to the magistrate. You are immediately seized and imprisoned."—Mr. M'Cheyne's speech to the Commission.

God help us when the Papists get into power here in our own dear country!

And what prodigious inroads they are now making, while our Churches and our people seem asleep in the boat, albeit the waves of danger are insidiously threatening it with destruction.

"Then if any follower of Mahomet came over to

the Christian faith, and openly confessed the Lord Jesus in his mouth, I am convinced that he would be put to death."

The way was perfectly open for them to preach the Gospel TO THE JEWS in the Holy Land; "but you were distinctly told that if you attempt to convert a single adherent of the Russian Greek Church, you would bring down on your head the vengeance of the Holy Synod and the vengeance of the Government."

"In Austria (Roman Catholic) the Government will suffer no missionaries. There we were treated with the utmost severity.

"All our Bibles—our English, our Hebrew, our German Bibles—were taken away, our papers were searched to see if they could discover whether we were missionaries, and what were our intentions. In that country it is out of the question to carry the Gospel to the poor misguided population.

"Popery exists in Cracow in its most disgusting form, and where we only found a single missionary to the Jews. I believe if that devoted missionary were to stand up and proclaim to the Roman Catholics the truth as it is in Jesus, he would be stoned to death before he could reach his own door."

Mr. M'Cheyne concluded with an earnest appeal to prosecute the mission to the Jews with the greatest vigour.

Mr. M'Cheyne, on arriving home, found a most gracious work of God going on in his church and neighbouring district.

The hearts and consciences of the people were

stirred to the very depths, and the Word of God was quick and powerful, and many were under concern about their souls.

Many private meetings were held—as many as thirty-nine were conducted weekly—AND FIVE OF THESE WERE CONDUCTED AND ATTENDED ENTIRELY BY CHILDREN, as I have already mentioned here.

Very few of the friends whom I knew in these early days are now left, and all the ministers of these times are also gone to their reward.

But what a savour of Christ they have left us! And in writing my sketches of these times, I have received numerous communications from friends, both at home and abroad, telling of the blessings of the Lord's goodness which they also had heard of or received in these early days of the gracious outpouring of His love and of His power.

O for the spirit of prayer again to our churches and our land, to our families and to ourselves!

O for an outpouring of the Holy Ghost on us Christians and on all! and O for the coming of the King, "whose right it is" (Ezek. xxi. 17).

Let us faithfully hold to Jesus and His Word, and God will bless us. Let us continue in prayer, and God will hear us. Let us plead the promises for blessing on this dead, dark, lost world, and God will rise for our help and give us "showers of blessing," as in the days of old.

"All nations whom Thou hast made shall come and worship before Thee, O Lord, and shall glorify Thy name" (Ps. lxxxvi. 9).

One day, somewhere, Mr. M'Cheyne was on a

coach with a young lady near him, and he asked her a question, when she replied, "I am a bishop's daughter."

"I wish you were a King's daughter," he said; and this remark was blessed by the Lord to her soul, so that after a time she wrote to him telling him that by grace she was now a "King's daughter." She had evidently given her heart to Jesus, as we are commanded, "My son, give Me thine heart" (Prov. xxiii. 26), "and let thine eyes observe My ways."—*Memoir*.

Sometimes a little, earnest, prayerful word is blessed to us all through our lives, as the above had been to the young lady. When Mr. W. C. Burns was reading *Pike's Early Piety*, which his father gave him, in one moment, while gazing on a solemn passage in it, his inmost soul was pierced as with a dart. God had apprehended him, and he poured out his heart for the first time with many tears and cries for mercy.

I at one time mentioned to a friend who had come from a distant land that I was writing about a minister who was once in Dundee, named M'Cheyne.

"My dear sir," he said, looking at me in an earnest way, "I have been reading M'Cheyne's books, and feeding on them for forty years."

On mentioning the above to another minister, "And so have I," he remarked. "Even in my unconverted days I read M'Cheyne."

"Since the 20th August 1839," wrote Mr. W. C. Burns about this time, "the church has been crowded every night, and many have been forced to go away without getting in. I hear daily many interesting evidences that the work of the Lord is going on through His own mighty power.

"Some of the greatest drunkards have been abstaining from day to day from their cups of poison that they may attend our meetings, and they appear to be daily receiving the deeper impressions. 'O Lord,' he continued, 'grant that these impressions may at last prove saving.'

"I was told of a man last night who, though previously ungodly, had been so much impressed by attending the meetings, that his wife, a godly woman, missing him the other morning at the breakfast hour, found him in the other room on his knees. And again waking at four in the morning, and missing him from his bed, she, rising, found him in the same room with his Bible in his hand.

"On Sabbath forenoon I preached," wrote Mr. Burns further, "with much of God's presence and power from John iv. 10, 'Jesus answered and said unto her, If thou knewest the gift of God, and who it is that saith to thee, Give Me to drink, thou wouldst have asked of Him, and He would have given thee living water.'"

Mr. Burns preached again in the afternoon with still greater liberty from Rom. viii. 34: "Who is he that condemneth? It is Christ that died, yea, rather, that is risen again, who is even at the right hand of God, who also maketh intercession for us."

"I never felt so powerfully," he wrote, "as in the afternoon, the absolute certainty of the believer's acceptance as righteous through Jesus, and the people appeared to be much impressed, though I have not yet heard of any new cases of awakening or conversion."

There was a meeting intimated to be held in the Meadows, Dundee (where the Albert Institute now stands), but as it was interdicted by the magistrates, it was held in St. Peter's Church graveyard, where a great number attended. In the evening a sermon was preached in the church by a minister from Edinburgh, from Ps. lxxxix. 15, "Blessed is the people that know the joyful sound; they shall walk, O Lord, in the light of Thy countenance."

"I think that the Spirit of God," he continues, "was much among the people of God on this occasion, filling them with joy and wonder at the free and infinite love of Jehovah."

One evening he prayed twice for an outpouring of the Spirit, after which there were many crying bitterly.

"One fell down," he wrote, "and when near the end I stopped and sat down in silent prayer for five minutes that all might be brought to the point of embracing Jesus, the feeling was intense, though most calm and solemn, and to believers very sweet."

Mr. Burns' meeting was interdicted; but there was a man about that time in Dundee—Rev. John Bowes —who preached in the open air, in spite of the magistrates.

He was several times taken before them and fined; although some of the best men in the town pleaded his cause, such as Mr. Edward Baxter, Mr. John Shiel and Mr. Patrick Watson, but without effect. Mr. Bowes wrote a severe letter to the magistrates after

all was over, concluding as follows:—"Hoping that
you will prepare to meet me before that August
tribunal of eternal justice, to which, from your decision, I appeal ; and praying that God may give you
repentance unto life,—I remain, your sincere friend,
JOHN BOWES."

Strange to say, two of his judges met with very
sudden deaths, and the third came to ruin in his
business. (See John Bowes' *Life*, pp. 268, 295.)

As it is Christlike to visit the sick and the dying,
one day in later years I entered a ward in the
Dundee Royal Infirmary.

For some little time there was not the slightest
noise, then an old man coughed very much, and my
guide whispered, "Consumption."

A nurse came in and wrapped up the limbs of a
child of eight years or so: the poor thing cried much.

Here is a man I know. His daughter sits by his
bed weeping.

She had been sent for to see her father ere he died.
He is not able to speak, but makes a sign to me of
recognition. He has some young ones at home, and
his wife is ill. She will not see her husband again
here, but he has sent a message that he hopes to
meet her in the end of the day.

I walk along. Ah, this is the orphan! How
changed he is, poor boy! Consumption here again—
sunken eyes, long thin fingers, wasting cough.

I have never seen a change so rapid. A printed
sheet of paper lies beside his bed. There are a few
Scripture promises on it—the sweet sayings of the
Lord.

"What is the matter, my boy?"

"A cold upon my lungs."

I asked if he had read and understood the words before him.

"Oh yes!" said he, "I understand them fine. You know I attended the Sabbath-school."

"And you had learned to pray there?"

"Yes; I pray morning and evening."

"That is right, my boy, and you will read those promises when you have time, and pray over them."

He held out his hand for the sheet, when I said, "Not now, but when you are able."

Speaking in whispers, he now said his mother was taken away when he was quite young, and his father the other year.

"Wouldn't it be a grand thing," I said, "if you are to be taken away too, if God would take you to heaven?"

"Ah, yes!" said he, smiling.

My heart yearned for the orphan, as, looking on him, I said, "Pray to Him to make you holy and take you there, and I will pray too."

He whispered, smiling again, "Thank you, sir. Good-bye."

I leave the Infirmary, and will heartily desire that our townsmen, rich and poor, may countenance and support this very useful Christian institution, and give it of their means, their presence, and their prayers.

In a few days the grave closed over the orphan.

Many summer suns and winter snows have since then passed and gone, but I still remember the little boy who learned to pray at the Sabbath-school, and

made the promises of his Heavenly Father his trust
and stay as he so early walked through the valley of
the shadow of death.

> The orphan rests his weary head
>   On his pillow in the ward,
> He knows the Saviour near his bed
>   Will his humble prayer regard :
> His life is fading hour by hour,
> " Christ will not get a withered flower."
>
> The orphan rests his weary soul
>   On his loving Saviour's breast :
> Jesus only maketh whole,
>   Jesus only giveth rest :
> His life is fading hour by hour,
> " Christ will not get a withered flower."
>
> The orphan rests now in his grave,
>   Daisies grow above his head ;
> He knows Immanuel's power to save,
>   The little orphan boy is dead :
> His life still faded hour by hour,
> Christ did not get a withered flower.

X

MR. M'CHEYNE went sometimes to visit a family living near Blairgowrie. One day when he was there a lady friend of mine called, and when she was leaving she was asked to "Come and shake hands with Mr. M'Cheyne." She was taken into the dining-room, which was his study during his visits, for he came from time to time for rest and quiet.

"I was delighted," she writes me, "to see the beautiful, heavenly expression of his face. We had no serious talk. I only stood beside him for a little, and do not remember anything he said. It was a pleasant incident, and his death so soon after impressed me deeply."

My friend further adds that several of the letters in his *Memoir* are addressed to the lady of the home whom she visited that day. Perhaps the excitement drove the minister's remarks from her memory.

One of the boys of the family having taken ill and died, Mr. M'Cheyne wrote some beautiful verses in memory of him, a few of which I give here:—

"I little thought, when last we met,
  Thy sun on earth was nearly set ;
I said what I can ne'er forget,
    'Dear boy, we'll meet again.'

> " The Sabbath sun rose bright and clear,
> When thine was setting on us here,
> To shine more bright in yonder sphere.
>   Farewell, we'll meet again.
>
> " I stood beside thy silent bed ;
> Thy marble brow was cold and dead ;
> Thy gentle soul was fled—was fled.
>   Dear boy, we'll meet again.
>
> " I saw thee in thy narrow rest,
> The clods upon thy coffin pressed,
> The clouds dropped tears ; yet in my breast
>   God said, ' We'll meet again.'
>
> " Yes, parents, smile through all your tears,
> A Crown of Life your darling wears ;
> The grave a shady porch appears,
>   To where we'll meet again.
>
> " The precious dust beneath that lies
> Shall at the call of Jesus rise
> To meet the Bridegroom in the skies,
>   That day we'll meet again."

You will see from the above verses how tender Mr. M'Cheyne's feelings were to the suffering and to the bereaved.

And there is a beautiful tribute paid to him by his friend, the late Rev. James Hamilton, of Regent Square, London, in the *Memoir*, namely :—" A striking characteristic of his piety was his absorbing love to the Lord Jesus. This was his ruling passion. It lightened all his labours, and made the reproaches which, for Christ's sake, sometimes fell on him by identifying him more and more with his suffering Lord, unspeakably precious. He cared for no question unless his Master cared for it, and his main

anxiety was to know the mind of Christ. He once
said to a friend, 'I bless God every morning I awake
that I live in witnessing times.'   If few congregations," continues Mr. Hamilton, " have witnessed the
scenes with which St. Peter's had become happily
familiar, one reason is that few ministers preach with
the fervour, the Christ-exalting simplicity, and the
prayerful expectancy of Robert M'Cheyne, and few
follow out their preaching with the yet more impressive urgency of his gracious intercourse and consistent
example."   (London, 3rd April 1843.)

Mr. M'Cheyne was enabled to go through
numerous and pressing engagements without hurry
or perturbation because of his tranquillity and com-
posure of spirit. He had the conscious knowledge
that he was the Lord's, and he committed his ways
to Him.

"We can discern," wrote Mr. Hamilton further,
" traces of this uniform self-possession in a matter so
minute as his handwriting. His most rapid notes
show no symptoms of haste or bustle, but end in
the same neat and regular style in which they began.
He proved that promise, 'Great peace have they
which love Thy law, and nothing shall offend them '
(Ps. cxix. 165)."

Those remarks are borne out from his signature,
very neatly written, in a small book now lying before
me, entitled *The Modern Traveller*, and the date is
27th March 1839, apparently the very day he left
Dundee for the Holy Land. For he wrote to his
parents in the steamboat a letter dated from ten
miles off the Nore, on 29th March 1839, 8 o'clock a.m.,

and saying, " Hitherto hath the Lord helped us," etc. It is probable that this small book was used by Mr. M'Cheyne during his long travels, as there are some of his markings on it in different places, and on page 43 he has written in pencil at the chapter, " Route from El Arisch to Jaffa," the words (very neatly), " 30, 31 May 1839." A lady to whom I sent some of these sketches very kindly sent me this interesting little volume as a present, and I now thank Mrs. Stirling very kindly for it.

Mr. M'Cheyne was very well educated, having entered the High School, Edinburgh, in October 1821, where he continued his literary studies for six years, and during the last year he composed a poem, entitled " Greece, but living Greece no more." Then he entered the Edinburgh University in November 1827, and gained some prizes in all the various classes he attended. He used his pencil very cleverly, and was able afterwards for the sketching of some scenes in Palestine. He was a very good singer, which enlivened his secret devotions, and enabled him to lead the song of praise in the congregation whenever occasion required, and his taste for poetry caused him to be adjudged the prize in Professor Wilson's class for a poem " On the Covenanters."

The death of his elder brother David was, as I have said, used by the Holy Spirit to be blessed to his soul. There can be no doubt that he himself looked upon the death of his brother David as the event which awoke him from the sleep of nature and brought in the first beam of Divine light into his soul. And in 1842 he, in writing to a friend, said, " This day, eleven years

ago, I lost my loved and loving brother, and began
to seek a Brother who cannot die."

At first the light dawned slowly, then we read :—
"*March* 11*th*, 1834. Read in the *Sum of Saving
Knowledge* (at the end of the Confession of Faith) the
work which I think first of all wrought a saving
change in me. How gladly would I renew the
reading of it if that change might be carried on to
perfection."

Friends may like to read a few sentences from his
diary, and as " the unholiness of his pleasures," the
Memoir adds, planted their stings in his heart, we
find him writing as follows :—

" *Sept.* 14*th*. May there be few such records as
this in my biography.

Again, " *Dec.* 9*th*. A thorn in my side—much
torment."

" *March* 10*th*, 1832. I hope never to play cards
again."

" *March* 25*th*. Never visit on a Sunday evening
again."

" *April* 10*th*. Absented myself from the dance ;
upbraidings ill to bear, but I must try to bear the
cross."

" *Nov.* 12*th*. Reading H. Martyn's *Memoirs*. Would
I could imitate him—giving up father, mother,
country, house, health, life, all for Christ. And yet,
what hinders ? Lord, purify me and give me strength
to dedicate myself, my all, to Thee.

" Reading Leigh Richmond's *Life*. Deep penitence,
not unmixed with tears. I never before saw myself
so vile, so useless, so poor, and, above all, so ungrate-

ful. May these tears be the pledge of my self-dedication."

Sometimes during the summer months Mr. M'Cheyne would have excursions into the country with some friend, and once they were caught in a Highland mist by which they had some trouble. He and a friend had set out on foot to explore at their leisure Dunkeld and its vicinity. They spent a day in that town, and about sunset set out again with the view of crossing the hills to Strathardle. A dense mist spread over the hills soon after they began to climb. They pressed on, but lost the track that might have guided them safely to the glen. They knew not how to direct their steps to any dwelling. Night came on, and they had no recourse but to crouch among the heath, with no other covering than the clothes they wore. They felt hungry and cold, and, awaking at midnight, the awful stillness of the lonely mountains spread a strange fear over them. But, drawing close together, they again lay down to rest, and slept soundly till the cry of some wild birds and the morning dawn aroused them. He may have had that excursion in mind when he wrote these beautiful verses at the Sea of Galilee :—

> "Fair are the lakes in the land I love,
>   Where pine and heather grow ;
>   But thou hast loveliness far above
>   What Nature can bestow.

> "It is not that the wild gazelle
>   Comes down to drink thy tide,
>   But He that was pierced to save from hell
>   Oft wandered by thy side."

I have had many letters from friends at home and abroad during the composition of these sketches, in appreciation of Mr. M'Cheyne and his godly life. One very interesting one came from a lady in Broughty - Ferry, and I will take the liberty of quoting it here :—

"I am much obliged for your kind thought of me in sending me your interesting sketch of Revival Times, and for your kind note. I read the enclosure with much pleasure, and return it with many thanks. May God indeed answer prayer that a similar time of blessed Revival may soon come to Dundee and neighbourhood again, also that many more like the sainted Mr. M'Cheyne may be raised for the true ministry of the Gospel, and the ingathering of souls."

Again from his journal :—

"*June 27th. Life of David Brainerd.* Most wonderful man. What conflicts, what depressions, desertions, strength, advancement, victories, within thy torn bosom. I cannot express what I think when I think of thee. To-night more set upon missionary enterprise than ever.

"*June 28th.* O for Brainerd's humility and sin-loathing dispositions!"

"*July 7th, Saturday.* After finishing my usual studies, tried to fast a little, with much prayer and earnest seeking of God's face, remembering what occurred this night last year" (alluding to his brother's death).

"*February 23rd, Sabbath.* Rose early to seek God, and found Him whom my soul loveth. Who would not rise early to meet such company? The rains are over and gone. They that sow in tears shall reap in joy."

"*June* 11*th*. After the example of Boston, whose *Life* I have been reading, examined my heart with prayer and fasting. It is the sweetest word in the Bible—'Sin *shall not* have dominion over you' (Rom. vi. 14)."

"*Sept.* 27*th*. Devoted chief part of Friday to fasting. Humbled and refreshed."

These solemn seasons and exercises made him have a care for a holy consistency in his daily walk. Aware that one idle word by a minister, one needless contention, one covetous act, *may destroy in our people the effect of many a solemn expostulation and earnest warning*, he was peculiarly circumspect in his every-day walk.

Baxter's words are not less than the truth :—" Recreation to a minister must be as whetting is with the mower—that is, only to be used as far as is necessary for his work. May a physician in the plague-time take any more relaxation or recreation than is necessary for his life when so many are expecting his help in a case of life and death? Will you stand by and see sinners gasping under the pangs of death, and say, 'God doth not require me to make myself a drudge to save them?' Is this the voice of ministerial or Christian compassion, or rather of sensual laziness and diabolical cruelty?"— *Memoir*, pp. 81, 82.

"*December* 31*st*. Young communicants. Two have made application to be admitted under eleven years of age, four that are only fourteen, three who are fifteen or sixteen."

"*January* 19*th*, 1840. (Communion.) There were six tables altogether. The people more and more moved to the end. At the last table every head seemed bent like a bulrush, while A.B. (Andrew Bonar) spoke of the ascension of Christ. Many of the little ones seemed deeply attentive. In the evening Mr. Burns preached in the school-room. When the church emptied, a congregation formed in the lower school and began to sing. Sang several psalms with them, and spoke on 'Behold, I stand at the door.' Altogether a day of the revelation of Christ—a sweet day to myself, and, I am persuaded, to many souls. Lord, make us meet for the table above."

One day, some years previous to this, Mr. M'Cheyne and Mr. Bonar had visited some of the miserable dwellings in Edinburgh. "Such scenes," he wrote, "I never before dreamed of. Ah, why am I such a stranger to the poor in my native town! What embedded masses of human beings are huddled together, unvisited by friend or minister! 'No man careth for our souls,' is written over every forehead. Awake, my soul, why should I give hours and days any longer to the vain world when there is such a world of misery at my very door. Lord, put Thine own strength in me, confirm every good resolution, forgive my past life of uselessness and folly." He forthwith began to work a district in the Canongate, teaching a Sabbath-school, and distributing the *Monthly Visitor.*

In Dundee there is much misery to be seen also,
I am sorry to say. I some time ago spoke to several
friends about a large number of very poor women
and young people who wait about for work. It was
really heartrending to see the squalor and misery.
A sad case having been reported to me at one time,
I called at a garret, off the High Street in Dundee,
up a number of stairs, where a poor woman was
lying on a low, dirty, wooden bedstead, the place
appearing altogether the very picture of adversity.
Her three young children were crouching about the
small fire-place, even the youngest appearing somewhat solemnly impressed with the desperate nature
of the case. The ceiling was much broken, freely
admitting the rain, and one or two large broken
dishes were placed here and there, catching the large
drops as they fell; and the wind blew through some
holes in the skylights, making the place cold and
dreary enough. I sat down on a chair beside this
poor young, dying wife, deserted by her hubsand, and
it was some little time before I could speak, the
misery around was so appalling. She coughed long
and loud as I sat there. " Poor thing, how are you
feeling?"   " Oh, I'm pretty well," she replied;
"you know I've given myself to Jesus." " I'm very
glad to hear it," I said. " When was that?" " Oh,
just when I lay down."   Much affected, I encouraged
her to trust in Him in life and death; then we had a
short prayer together that our Father would for His
Son's sake sustain and save this dear soul. She told
me some kind neighbours did any little thing for her,
and the " Board" was helping her. " You are calm

and happy like," I said when next I saw her. "I'm just resting on the Saviour," she replied. The children were looking better and cleaner, having been under the care of a kind neighbour for some days. The last time I saw her she was very spent, but calm and happy. I said, "The Lord will take care of your children." She wept, and then said in a whisper, "Oh yes." "Dear friend," I asked, "are you still relying on Jesus." "Yes, yes," she whispered, as I pressed her hand and said "Good-bye." Next visit the children were sitting round the fire, a neighbour beside them, and a white cover was spread over the bed. She undid the sheet, and the wasted face was exposed for a few moments of this believing woman now entered into her rest. A Christian brother and I saw her laid in the grave. Although her husband deserted her, Jesus did not.

> "Earthly friends may pain and grieve thee,
> One day kind, the next day leave thee;
> But this Friend will ne'er deceive thee,
> O, how He loves!"

XI

A T the foot of Mount Lebanon, in the town of Beyrout, Mr. M'Cheyne, when on his way from visiting Jerusalem, expounded Acts x. at a prayer-meeting of the American Missionary Brethren, at which he was well pleased, because he had been feeling ill, and was thankful to be somewhat restored to the work again. But, having paid a visit to a young man from Glasgow in that town (Beyrout), who was ill of fever, he seemed to be seized with the same illness, and was very soon prostrated under it. "One day," writes Dr. Bonar, who was with him, "his spirit revived and his eye glistened when I spoke of the Saviour's sympathy, adducing as the very words of Jesus, Ps. xli. 1: 'Blessed is he that considereth the poor: the Lord will deliver him in time of trouble,' etc.

"It seemed so applicable to his own case, as a minister of the Glad Tidings, for often had he considered the poor, carrying a cup of cold water to a disciple. Another passage, written for the children of God in their distress, was spoken to him when he seemed nearly insensible: 'Call upon me in the day of trouble' (Ps. l. 15). This word of God was as the drop of honey to Jonathan."

"My mind was very weak," Mr. M'Cheyne wrote,

"when I was at the worst, and therefore the things of eternity were often dim.   I really believed that my Master had called me home, and that I would sleep beneath the dark green cypresses of Bonja till the Lord shall come, and they that sleep in Jesus come with Him, and my most earnest prayer was for my dear flock, that God would give them a pastor after His own heart."—*Memoir*, p. 114.

Mr. M'Cheyne's prayer was not unavailing.   God looked on his flock in St Peter's, Dundee, in His great love, and opened the windows of heaven and poured down a most gracious blessing, so that there was scarcely room to receive it, for it overflowed to all the neighbourhood, and its fragrance is felt in the Christian world to this day.

On the 23rd July 1839, Mr. M'Cheyne's assistant in St. Peter's Church, the Rev. W. C. Burns, had been out at Kilsyth, a village near Glasgow, preaching for his father, who was the minister there, and while he was pressing on the congregation with deep solemnity the necessity of their immediate acceptance of the Lord Jesus Christ to be their Saviour, the whole of the vast assembly were overpowered.   "The Holy Spirit seemed as a rushing mighty wind" (Acts ii. 2) to fill the place.   Very many were that day struck to the heart, and the sanctuary was filled with distressed and enquiring souls.   All Scotland heard the glad news—that the sky was no longer as brass, that the rain had now begun to fall.   The Spirit in mighty power began to work from that day forward in many places of the land.

On the 8th of August Mr. Burns returned to

Dundee, and two days after the Spirit began to work in St. Peter's at the congregational prayer-meeting in the church in a similar way as at Kilsyth. Mr. Burns tells the following interesting cases at this time:—He speaks of a man who comes regularly to St. Peter's from Long Forgan, a distance of five miles, and that the origin of it is very remarkable. One day in winter this man and a companion were working in a quarry, and happened to be beside a fire, when a person came up on a pony, and for what reason they did not know came off and went up to them. He entered into conversation on the state of their souls, drawing some alarming truths from the blazing fire. The men were surprised, and said—

"Ye're nae common man."

"Oh yes," says he, "just a common man."

One of the men, however, recognised him as Mr. M'Cheyne, and they were so much impressed that one of them has been coming regularly to St. Peter's. His mother hopes that he is really a converted man, and she told Mr. Burns that he has been for some time a member of a prayer-meeting. "What a striking lesson," Mr. Burns adds, "to be instant in season and out of season" (2 Tim. iv. 2).

This woman had another son who became ill, and was brought under conviction of sin, and had dark and despairing views for a long time, and would often cry like a child. One day he appeared as if rising from the green, where he had been, as she thought, in prayer, coming into the house with a smiling countenance. They were amazed, and asked the reason. "Oh, mother," said he, "I see that there is more merit in the blood of Jesus than there is guilt in my sins, and why should I fear!" This brought tears of joy into all their eyes. He afterwards died in peace—the peace of God in believing the Gospel.

Mr. Burns began a series of discourses in St. Peter's on Ps. cxxx., and writes:—"I was much supported all day, and had nearer views of the holiness of Jehovah than ever before in the pulpit. Two prayer-meetings have been begun among the young women; those among the older people are becoming larger and more lively."

It might be nice to give here the beautiful hymn about Jehovah by Isaac Watts:—

> " Before Jehovah's awful throne,
>   Ye nations, bow with sacred joy;
> Know that the Lord is God alone,
>   He can create, and He destroy.
>
> " His sovereign power, without our aid,
>   Made us of clay and formed us men;
> And when, like wandering sheep, we strayed,
>   He brought us to His fold again.
>
> " We'll crowd Thy gates with thankful songs,
>   High as the heavens our voices raise;
> And earth, with her ten thousand tongues,
>   Shall fill Thy courts with sounding praise.
>
> " Wide as the world is Thy command,
>   Vast as eternity Thy love,
> Firm as a rock Thy Truth must stand,
>   While rolling years shall cease to move."

At that time, about 1839, there was a young man teaching a school at Invergowrie, but had been a

sailor and made several voyages abroad, whose name
was Thomas Alexander. He was led to St. Peter's
Church, and under the ministry of Mr. M'Cheyne he
largely imbibed the spirit of his pastor. He went to
college, became a minister, and was ultimately settled
as pastor of the Presbyterian Church in Chelsea,
where the Earl of Dalhousie and several of the
Scotch members of Parliament attended his services,
and he had the honour of being elected the Moderator
of the English Presbyterian Synod some years before
his death. I heard him at one time preach in Free
St. David's, Dundee, very beautifully from Ps.
lxviii. 13: "Walk about Zion, and go round about
her; tell the towers thereof. Mark ye well her
bulwarks, consider her palaces, that ye may tell it
to the generation following." He told us how the
Gospel was adapted for the meanest capacity, and
that one time he was in the English Lake district
when he observed an idiot woman. As he was about
the doors, he thought he would try an experiment
how far she could understand the salvation of God,
and took pains to instruct her accordingly. She
took an illness, and he saw her frequently, still instructing her to the best of his ability in the things
of the Kingdom. One night he was called to see her,
as if she were dying. He sat a long time beside her,
then rose to slip away, when she cried out to him,
and he sat down for a long time again. Then, when
the morning was dawning, she pulled herself up in
bed by a rope which hung there for her convenience,
pointed upward with her hand, crying out, "Christ
there"; then she pointed to her heart and cried out,

"Christ there," after which she let go the rope, fell back, and died.

A friend and I visited Mr. Alexander in Chelsea at one time. He was the author of a Commentary on the 51st Psalm, *The Penitent's Prayer.* I have this work now lying before me. The author gives the Psalm in several metrical pieces, by Mary, Countess of Pembroke, about 1570; Miles Coverdale, 1549; W. Hunnis, 1550; Francis Rous, 1646; George Withers, 1632; George Sandys, 1636; Richard Baxter, 1692. The author adds, on Dr. Chalmers' *Daily Scripture Readings*:—"This is the most deeply affecting of all the psalms, and I am sure the one most applicable to me." To conclude on this most interesting psalm, I have looked up in my large copy of old John Trapp, the Commentator, 1657, and find the following on the words in the 17th verse: "A broken and a contrite heart, O God, Thou wilt not despise," which I pray may be blessed to some readers, as the old saying is still true, that any text which has done YOU good, will be blessed to others by the power of sympathy and, of course, the blessing of God accorded to it.

"There is great comfort," writes Trapp, "to those that droop under sense of sin and fear of wrath, being at next door to despair.

"Bring but a broken heart and God will receive you graciously, pouring the oil of His grace into your broken vessels.

"This comforted Bernard on his death-bed: he died with this sentence in his mouth.

"Austin caused it to be written on the wall

over-against his bed, where he lay sick, and died.

"Many poor souls, even in times of Popery, had heaven opened unto them by meditating upon this psalm, and especially on this seventeenth verse."

The Rev. Thomas Alexander was also the author of *Discourses on Christ's Intercessory Prayer*, and a biographical sketch of the Rev. W. C. Burns, to whom I refer in these articles on revivals.

Mr. Alexander Somerville, afterwards minister of Anderston Church, Glasgow, was Mr. M'Cheyne's familiar friend and companion in the gay scenes of their youth. But he was also, about the same time, brought to the knowledge of Christ, and so they united their efforts for each other's welfare, and met together for the study of the Bible, and used to· exercise themselves in the Septuagint Greek and the Hebrew original. But oftener still they met in prayer and solemn converse, and carrying on all their studies in the same spirit, and watched each other's steps in the narrow way.

Mr. M'Cheyne's diary (see *Memoir*) :—*December 9th.* "Heard a street preacher, foreign voice; seems really in earnest. He quoted the striking passage: 'The Spirit and the Bride say Come, and let him that heareth say Come' (Rev. xxii. 17). From this he seems to derive his authority. Let me learn from this man to be in earnest for the Truth, and to despise the scoffing of the world."

About this time he seems to have been deeply affected by hearing that a lady friend of the family had said "that she was determined to keep by the world," and he wrote some verses on the subject:—

> "She hath chosen the world
>   And its paltry crowd;
> She hath chosen the world
>   And an endless shroud;
> She hath chosen the world
>   With its misnamed pleasures;
> She hath chosen the world
>   Before Heaven's own treasures.

> "She hath launched her boat
>   On life's giddy sea,
> And her all is afloat
>   For eternity;
> But Bethlehem's star
>   Is not in her view,
> And her aim is far
>   From the Harbour true.

> "When the storm descends
>   From an angry sky;
> Ah! where from the winds
>   Shall the vessel fly?
> When stars are concealed
>   And rudder gone,
> And heaven is sealed
>   To the wandering one.

> "Away, then! O fly
>   From the joys of earth!
> Her smile is a lie,
>   There's a sting in her mirth.
> Come, leave the dreams
>   Of this transient night,
> And bask in the beams
>   Of an endless Light."

June 25th.—In reference to the office of the holy ministry, he wrote:—"Men set apart to the work, chosen out of the chosen, as it were, the very pick of the flocks, who are to shine as the stars for ever and ever. Alas! alas! my soul, where shalt thou appear? O Lord God! I am a little child, but thou wilt send an angel with a live coal from off the altar and touch my unclean lips, and put a tongue within my dry mouth, so that I shall say with Isaiah, 'Here am I; send me.'"

"*March 6th.*—Wild wind and rain all day long. Hebrew class. Psalms. New beauty in the original every time I read. Dr. Welsh lectures on Pliny's letter about the Christians of Bithynia; Professor Jameson on quartz; Dr. Chalmers grappling with Hume's arguments."

"*April 8th.*—Have found much rest in Him who bore all our burdens for us."

"*May 6th.*—Saturday evening." This was the evening previous to the Communion, and in prospect of again declaring himself the Lord's at His table, he enters into a brief review of his state. He had partaken of the ordinance in May of the year before for the first time, but he was then living at ease, and saw not the solemn nature of the step he took.

I would like to give a notice here of the beautiful Communion service in our Scotch Presbyterian Church, but will only take time to refer to the first service after I was ordained an elder in April 1856. We had a dear old man of God in the session, one of our senior elders, who welcomed us newly-ordained juniors to the work of God in the congregation; and our first Communion season was held as I had been appointed session-clerk. This aged friend was the

late Dean of Guild William Curr, Dundee, of whom
the Curr Night Refuge is his memorial to this day.
Having thus been associated with him as an elder
of the Free Church of Scotland, I had many opportunities of estimating his character and of admiring
the intelligent, humble, holy walk by which he was
distinguished.   I think he truly adorned the doctrine
of God our Saviour.   As a business man he was
much respected, and after a long and prosperous
career he was elected to this honourable position in
our town, the duties of·which he discharged with
dignity and respect.   He had long sat under the
ministry of the Rev. George Lewis, who was a friend
of the children, a leader in the cause of education,
in endeavouring to raise the poor to comfort and
self-respect, and with honest indignation to declaim
against the ravages which the public-house made upon
the souls, bodies, and homes of its unhappy victims ;
and our aged friend sympathised to the last in the
practical philosophy of his worthy pastor.   The loss
of an only child, a very promising young man, was
a sore trial to him, but he got strength for the burden,
and was able to bear it in meekness and submission.

> " If thou should'st call me to resign
>   What most I prize : it ne'er was mine ;
>   I only yield Thee what is Thine—
>   Thy will be done."

One of his oft-repeated sayings was—" The Lord
loveth a cheerful giver" (2 Cor. ix. 7), and no
doubt it was spoken from the heart, as he appeared
to act on that principle while in public, and in private
he was engaged in endless acts of charity.

We had just enjoyed a happy Communion season in Free St. David's, Dundee, when it was suddenly reported that he was taken ill. I called and found him in a very weak state and in bed. I was kindly invited into his room, and saw him. I felt awed and moved to see one whom I had long looked on with respect and admiration now, to all appearance, on his death-bed. How the mind is solemnised when looking on a dying Christian! How does he feel with eternity at hand? How can he calmly part with near and dear ones? What is the ground of his confidence?

Ah! it is Jesus who gives the peace in that serious hour. "When thou passest through the waters, I will be with thee; and through the rivers, they shall not overflow thee. When thou walkest through the fire, thou shalt not be burned, neither shall the flame kindle upon thee" (Isa. xliii. 2, 3). I read the Scriptures with him and prayed. He seemed calm and resigned. It was like him to bear in meekness the holy will of his Heavenly Father, for "He giveth grace to the humble" (1 Pet. v. 5). He was not able to speak much, but quietly listened to the Word of God while I read to him as he lay a-dying. His kind wife, with watchful care, tended him and helped him with her loving ways in his moments of weakness, while the sympathy of many a sincere and grateful friend was heartily accorded them both.

> "Vital spark of heavenly flame!
> Quit, O quit, this mortal frame!
> Trembling, hoping, lingering, flying,
> O the pain, the bliss of dying!
> Cease, fond nature, cease thy strife,
> And let me languish into Life."

> "The world recedes, it disappears,
>   Heaven opens on my eyes ; my ears
>   With sounds seraphic ring.
>   Lend, lend your wings ; I mount, I fly ;
>   O grave ! where is thy victory ?
>   O death ! where is thy sting ? "

And thus this aged father and esteemed friend passed away and departed to be with Christ, which is far better. "For we know that if our earthly house of this tabernacle were dissolved, we have a building of God, an house not made with hands, eternal in the heavens" (2 Cor. v. 1).

An old lady visited me on the 20th October 1906, she being a convert of M'Cheyne's, but she was never at the Communion table along with him. She was in the country when Mr. M'Cheyne held his communicants' class, and then he could not take her the next time because he was ill and not able to have another communicants' class. She was weeping bitterly, and he said, "It's only three months, Jane, to the next Communion"; but she replied, "We might be all in our graves by the three months, and I take it as a token that I shall never sit down at the Communion table with you." She was very much disappointed. He came to the door with her, and patted her in sympathy on the shoulder at parting.[1]

[1] This narrative is continued in the next chapter.

XII

"THE holy man," said my aged friend to me, as she told me this story lately, "the sight of him broke my heart. I could just weep, such a sinner I was." She was very sorry for saying these things to Mr. M'Cheyne that day, and, strange to say, she really never was at the Communion table with him, as he died soon after their interview.

She had found peace and was happy about this time, and as Dr. Horatius Bonar took charge of the young communicants in St. Peter's Church after Mr. M'Cheyne's death, my friend Jane was admitted then for the first time to the table of the Lord. " I believed in Jesus," she said, "and trusted Him, and so the Spirit made me free; for if ye know the truth, 'the truth shall make you free'" (John viii. 32). "So the Lord enabled me," she continued, "for many years to speak to anxious souls, and it has been glorious work."

At her first Communion she was confused in her mind, and does not remember much about it. "Sometimes Mr. M'Cheyne would preach till five o'clock on Sabbath afternoon, and when he would say 'Lastly' there would be a thrill go through me, and I would say, 'Oh dear, is he going to stop?' as I could have stayed all night to hear him." Thus we may say that the Divine promise of God was fulfilled in Mr. M'Cheyne, namely—"And I will give you pastors according to Mine heart, which shall feed you with knowledge and understanding" (Jer. iii. 15).

There are a few nice verses on this subject in the 119th Psalm, which I like (vers. 33–37):—

> " Teach me, O Lord, the perfect way
>   Of Thy precepts divine,
> And to observe it to the end
>   I shall my heart incline.
> Give understanding unto me,
>   So keep Thy law shall I ;
> Yea, ev'n with my whole heart, I shall
>   Observe it carefully.
>
> " In Thy law's path make me to go,
>   For I delight therein.
> My heart unto Thy testimonies,
>   And not to greed incline.
> Turn Thou away my sight and eyes
>   From viewing vanity ;
> And in Thy good and holy way
>   Be pleased to quicken me."

It will be observed by the incident which I have related here that Mr. M'Cheyne was very particular about the Sacrament, and he wrote a beautiful little tract on that subject, entitled "This do in remembrance of Me."

"The Lord's Supper is the sweetest of all ordinances," he wrote, "because of the time when it was instituted, 'the same night in which He was betrayed.' The Lord's Supper is the children's bread; it is intended only for those who know and love the Lord Jesus. When a bride accepts the right hand in

marriage before many witnesses, it is a solemn
declaration to all the world that she does accept the
bridegroom to be her only husband. So, in the
Lord's Supper, when you receive that bread and wine,
you solemnly declare that, forsaking all others, you
heartily do receive the Lord Jesus as your only Lord
and Saviour.   Some of you know that you are living
under the power of sins that you could name, secret
profanation of the holy Sabbath, in secret swearing,
or lying, or dishonesty, or drinking, or unclean-
ness.

"Ah! why should you feed on this bread and
wine? It will do you no good. Can you for a
moment doubt that you will eat and drink un-
worthily?   Dare you do this?"

How lovely it is to be at the Table of the Lord!
How sweet to feel true love and gratitude glowing in
our hearts to the dear Saviour! Such peace it brings
to think of Him who died for us and rose again—
"His praise be ever new."   And many friends at
home and abroad, as they read the following verses,
may be reminded of the happy moments they have
had there, with dear ones beside them, who have now
fallen asleep in Jesus, to be for ever with the Lord :—

> " 'Twas on that night, when doom'd to know
> The eager rage of ev'ry foe,
> That night in which He was betray'd,
> The Saviour of the world took bread ;
> And, after thanks and glory giv'n
> To Him that rules in earth and heav'n,
> That symbol of His flesh He broke,
> And thus to all His followers spoke :

" My broken body thus I give
    For you, for all ; take, eat, and live ;
    And oft the sacred rite renew,
    That brings My wondrous love to view.
    Then in His hands the cup He rais'd,
    And God anew He thank'd and praised ;
    While kindness in His bosom glow'd,
    And from His lips salvation flow'd :

" My blood I thus pour forth, He cries,
    To cleanse the soul in sin that lies :
    In this the covenant is seal'd,
    And Heav'n's eternal grace reveal'd.
    With love to man this cup is fraught,
    Let all partake the sacred draught ;
    Through latest ages let it pour,
    In mem'ry of My dying hour."

Paraphrase xxxv.

When Mr. M'Cheyne was on his journey to Palestine, he frequently speaks about his sacramental services in his church in St. Peter's, Dundee.

To his sister Eliza, who was a member of our Prayer Union, and with whom I corresponded a little, he wrote from Genoa :—" My dear people, and all of you, have been much on my heart during these days, and you may be sure I am anxious to know how the Sacrament was conducted in St. Peter's, how all my friends were helped in their services, and if there were marks of good done to perishing souls. Ah, dear Eliza, every step I take, and every new country I see, makes me feel more that there is nothing real, nothing true, but what is everlasting ! Happy you and I, dear Eliza, if we have part in Christ, for we shall stand with Him in glory when all the world shall sink

in ruins. At four in the morning we sailed again to
Arles, and then in another steamer still further down
the Rhone. We grieved thus to use the Lord's day,
but felt it a case of necessity, and tried to make good
use of our time. We soon gave tracts to all on board,
mostly French, one German, one Italian, one English
—all received them very anxiously, rich and poor,
passengers and sailors. It was my sacramental day
in St. Peter's, and my heart was with my flock. It
was a lovely sunshine morning."

"Balteen, 19th May.—Spent our Sabbath unoccupied in midst of the village. The poor Arabs
have no Sabbath. It was sweet to rest and remember
you all in the wilderness. Reached San about ten in
the morning. This evening we spent in exploring
the ruins of the ancient Zoan, for this, we find, is the
very spot. Wandered alone. We were much surprised
to find great mounds of brick and pottery and vitrified
stones. Andrew (Bonar) at last came upon some
beautiful obelisks.

"In the morning we examined all carefully, found
two sphinxes and many Egyptian obelisks. How
wonderful to be treading over the ruins of the ancient
capital of Egypt. 'Where are the princes of Zoan?'
(Isa. xix. 12). 'God has set fire in Zoan' (Ezek.
xiii. 14). This is the very place where Joseph was
sold a slave, and where Moses did his wonders
(Ps. lxxviii. 12–43).

> "'Things marvellous He brought to pass;
> Their fathers them beheld,
> Within the land of Egypt done,
> Yea, even in Zoan's field.

" ' Nor how great signs in Egypt land
          He openly had wrought :
    What miracles in Zoan's field
          His hand to pass had brought.'

"This was almost the only place where we have been in danger from the inhabitants. Dr. Black preached yesterday, before sailing, in the American Consul's. We had the Communion afterwards at the Mission House. It was pleasant to join in that holy service with so many of different persuasions. There were more than twenty Turbans — two that had been Armenian bishops, with venerable beards—one Abyssinian, several Greek Catholics, Presbyterians, Congregational, and Church of Scotland, and four converted Jews. I fear I shall not be back till the end of October, if all shall go on safely, so that I must devolve my Communion again on some of my friends."—M'Cheyne's *Familiar Letters*.

"Many will remember for ever," writes Mr. M'Cheyne's biographer, "the blessed Communion Sabbaths that were enjoyed in St. Peter's. From the very first, these Communion sermons were remarkably owned of God. The awe of His presence used to be upon His people, and the house filled with the odour of the ointment when His name was poured forth."

I would like to tell my readers how the sacramental services were conducted fifty years ago. The Thursday previous was set apart by the people of God as a day of humiliation and prayer, and the churches were filled somewhat as on a Sabbath day. On Saturday there were services in the afternoon in

the churches as a preparation for the coming day.
Then dawned upon us the blessed Communion
Sabbath, with its peace and rest and joy in the
Lord, sweet type of the eternal Sabbath to be
enjoyed by us with the Lord Jesus in glory. "O
that every day was a Sabbath," said a dear minister
once, "and every Sabbath a Communion day!"
Thus may we all pass our short, brief lives, then be
for ever with the Lord.

> "Hunger and thirst are felt no more,
>   Nor suns with scorching ray,
> God is their sun, whose cheering beams
>   Diffuse eternal day.
>
> "'Mong pastures green He'll lead His flock,
>   Where living streams appear;
> And God the Lord from ev'ry eye
>   Shall wipe off ev'ry tear."   *Paraphrase* lxvi.

It was nice for the elders to meet with the minister
in the Session-house before the services commenced
on these Sabbath mornings to pray together for the
Divine blessing, and many a sweet meeting I have
enjoyed there.

Then in the church the psalm would be sung, the
prayers offered to the Lord, and the sermon might
tell of the Saviour's wonderful love, to pour out His
blood for us on Calvary's rugged tree.

The symbols of that love would then be brought
forward by the elders, while the beautiful verses which
I have already given here would be sung by the
congregation to the tune of "Communion," with
melting solemnity :—

" With love to man this cup is fraught,
    Let all partake the sacred draught ;
    Through latest ages let it pour,
    In mem'ry of My dying hour."

Bread and wine are only symbols
    Of the Saviour's dying love :
Go, believer, serve Him gladly,
    Till you meet with Him above.

After the minister had served the symbols of His dying love, there was a solemn pause. Many hearts were dealing with the Saviour; some, perhaps, determining by grace to love and serve Him more; others saying a word to Him for dear ones beside them or far away; and perhaps solemn vows would be made, in the strength of the Lord, to live more for Christ, and souls, and eternity. The parting moment at the table came, and all would join in singing some verses of the 103rd Psalm, dear to the people of God over the whole world, perhaps to the tune of " Martyrdom " or " St. David " :—

"O thou my soul, bless God the Lord :
    And all that in me is
Be stirred up His holy name
    To magnify and bless.
Bless, O my soul, the Lord thy God,
    And not forgetful be
Of all His gracious benefits
    He hath bestow'd on thee."

Afterwards came prayer and exhortation, or perhaps reading the twelfth chapter of Romans, a few verses of which I might give here :—

" I beseech you therefore, brethren, by the mercies of God, that ye present your bodies a living sacrifice, holy, acceptable unto God, which is your reasonable service.

"And be not conformed to this world; but be ye transformed by the renewing of your mind, that ye may prove what is that good, and acceptable, and perfect will of God.

"For I say, through the grace given unto me, to every man that is among you, not to think of himself more highly than he ought to think; but to think soberly, according as God hath dealt to every man the measure of faith. . . .

"Let love be without dissimulation. Abhor that which is evil; cleave to that which is good.

"Be kindly affectioned one to another with brotherly love; in honour preferring one another;

"Not slothful in business; fervent in spirit; serving the Lord;

"Rejoicing in hope; patient in tribulation; continuing instant in prayer;

"Distributing to the necessity of saints; given to hospitality.

"Bless them which persecute you: bless, and curse not.

"Rejoice with them that do rejoice, and weep with them that weep. . . .

"Be not overcome of evil, but overcome evil with good."

Then the congregation, perhaps standing, would sing to the tune of "St. Paul's" the 122nd Psalm, 6th to 9th verses, and, with the pastor's blessing, conclude the blessed services of the day :—

> "Pray that Jerusalem may have
>   Peace and felicity :
> Let them that love thee and thy peace
>   Have still prosperity,

"Therefore I wish that peace may still
        Within thy walls remain,
    And ever may thy palaces
        Prosperity retain.

"Now, for my friends' and brethren's sakes,
        Peace be in thee, I'll say,
    And for the house of God our Lord,
        I'll seek thy good alway."

Thus was the Communion generally held in the olden time, when reviving and quickening grace was abundantly poured out upon the people of God, that they might love the Saviour more and serve Him better.

After prayer I have thought I might humbly just tell what is in my own diary for the first Communion Sabbath after I was ordained an elder by my minister, the Rev. Charles Nairn, of Free St. David's Church, Dundee. This was some time after our first Disruption minister, the Rev. George Lewis, had been transferred from our church to Ormiston, near Edinburgh. Mr. Lewis kindly came to our first Communion after the new elders' ordination :—

"*Sabbath, 20th April*, 1856.—This is Communion Sabbath; have had much spiritual blessing to-day.

"Felt the Saviour precious to my soul. Was at the second table, and served by Mr. Lewis.

"Our friends were all served same time.

"Served cups at third and bread at fourth table, and was enabled to go through it well.

"Mr. Lewis preached in the evening from John xxi. 9: 'As soon then as they were come to land, they saw a fire of coal there, and fish laid thereon, and bread,' showing us that Christ minded men's bodies as well as their souls, by having a fire kindled and fish on it ready for the disciples when they came ashore from their work, and showed how Christ would welcome the redeemed soul on the shores of eternity.

"At the table I praised Him for many temporal and spiritual mercies, remembered poor Mrs. Bell (a dying woman), and James Talbert (a well-known man of God, an invalid in Dundee) by name to Him.

"Asked blessings to my minister; asked spiritual blessings to the people; remembered all my friends at the table by name, and had much peace."

Now these dear ministers and elders and many friends are all gone to the rest that remaineth to the people of God (Heb. iv. 9), and may we who are yet on earth still follow on to know the Lord, and seek, as the Bible hymn says, to have loving, cheerful hearts to taste all his gifts with joy.

> "Through every period of my life
> Thy goodness I'll proclaim,
> And after death, in distant worlds,
> Resume the glorious theme.

> "When nature fails, and day and night
> Divide Thy works no more,
> My ever-grateful heart, O Lord,
> Thy mercy shall adore.

> "Through all eternity to Thee
> A joyful song I'll raise,
> For oh! eternity's too short
> To utter all Thy praise."

XIII

MR. M'CHEYNE had not been many months engaged in his laborious work in Dundee when he was solicited to remove to the parish of Skirling, near Biggar (see *Memoir*). But he wrote to his father :—" I dare not leave three or four thousand people (in his parish) for three hundred. Had this been offered me before, I would have seen it a direct intimation from God, and would heartily have embraced it. How I should have delighted to feed so precious a little flock—to watch over every family— to know every heart—to allure to brighter worlds and lead the way. But God has not so ordered it. He has set me down among the noisy mechanics and political weavers of this godless town. Perhaps the Lord will make this wilderness of chimney tops to be green and beautiful as the garden of the Lord, a field which the Lord hath blessed."

At the close of 1837 he agreed to become secretary to the Church Extension Scheme in the county of Forfar, to bring to overgrown parishes the advantage of a faithful minister placed over a number of souls as he could really visit. "Many a time have I prayed," he wrote, "that God would open the hearts of our rulers to feel that their highest duty and greatest glory is to support the ministers of Christ, and to send these to every perishing soul in Scotland."

He rejoiced greatly in the settlement of faithful ministers, and the appointments of Mr. Baxter to Hilltown church, the Rev. George Lewis to St. David's, and Mr. Miller to Wallacetown, Dundee, at a later period, are all noticed by him with expressions of thankfulness and joy. And when the Rev. Andrew Bonar was ordained at Collace, September 20th, 1838, he was present with great joy, and wrote: "Blessed be God for the gift of this pastor. Give testimony to the word of Thy grace."

Mr. M'Cheyne's prayerfulness and waiting on the Lord for wisdom and guidance is again observable in the case of his having been strongly urged to preach as a candidate for the vacant parish of St. Martin's, near Perth, and assured of the appointment if he would only come forward. But he declined again, and wrote: "My Master has placed me here with His own hand, and I never will directly nor indirectly seek to be removed." He wrote also to Rev. Andrew Bonar about this case on 8th August 1837, which shows how he prayed and looked to the Lord for guidance: "I was much troubled about being asked to go to a neighbouring parish at present vacant, and made it a matter of prayer, and I mention it now because of the wonderful answer to prayer which I think I received from God. I prayed that, in order to settle my own mind completely about staying, He would awaken some of my people. I agreed that that would be a sign He would wish me to stay. The next morning, I think, or at least the second morning, there came to me two young persons I had never seen before, in great distress. What brought this to my mind was that they came to me again yesterday, and their distress is greatly increased. Indeed, I never saw any people in such anguish about their soul. I cannot but regard this as a real answer to prayer. I have also several other persons in deep distress, and I feel that I am quite helpless in comforting them. I would fain be like Noah, who put out his hand and took in the weary dove; but God makes me stand by and feel that I am a child. Pray for me, for my people, for my own soul, that I be not a castaway."

How refreshing it is, I would say, to hear this dear minister speaking in this way about prayer, and waiting on God, who is the hearer and answerer of prayer.

> " Prayer makes the darkening cloud withdraw;
> Prayer climbs the ladder Jacob saw,
> Gives exercise to faith and love,
> Brings every blessing from above.

> " Restraining prayer, we cease to fight;
> Prayer keeps the Christian's armour bright;
> And Satan trembles when he sees
> The weakest saint upon his knees."

Although Mr. M'Cheyne was very busy at home, he scarcely ever refused an invitation to preach on a week day, as his *Memoir* mentions. It would be difficult even to enumerate the places which he watered at Communion seasons, and it was said of him that not the words he spoke, but the holy manner in which he spoke, was the chief means of arresting souls.

His ways were thus "lovely and of godly report" (Phil. iv. 8), both of which add power and graciousness to every Christian, and are indispensable to the character of every true and faithful minister of Christ. Another prayerful plan was when Mr. Andrew Bonar, of Collace, and Mr. M'Cheyne, of Dundee, would meet together to spend the whole day in confession of ministerial and personal sins, with prayer for grace, guiding themselves by the reading of the Word.

"At such times," Mr. Bonar wrote, "we used to meet in the evening with the flock of the pastor in whose house the meetings had been held through the day, and then unitedly pray for the Holy Spirit being poured down upon the people. The first time we held such a meeting there were tokens of blessing observed by several of us, and the week after Mr. M'Cheyne wrote:—'Has there been any fruit of the happy day we spent with you? I thought I saw some the Sabbath after here.' 'In due season we shall reap if we faint not,' 'only be thou strong and of a good courage.'"

The incident that encouraged him is recorded in his diary, namely: "An elderly person came to tell him how the river of joy and peace in believing had that Sabbath most singularly flowed through her soul, so that she blessed God that ever she came to St. Peter's. This seems," he adds, "a fruit of our prayer-meeting begun last Wednesday at Collace— one drop of the shower."

"This is the noblest science," he wrote, "to know how to live in hourly communion with God in Christ." May you and I know more of this, and thank God we are not among the ' wise and prudent from whom these things are hid.'"

"Thou to the pure and lowly heart
Hast heavenly truth revealed,
Which, from the self-conceited mind,
Thy wisdom hath concealed.

"Come then to Me, all ye who groan,
With guilt and fears opprest;
Resign to Me the willing heart,
And I will give you rest."

"I was taken to St. Peter's Church," writes Miss Sime, a lady friend, to me, "when I was very young, the first day it was opened. But my memory only goes back to revival days, when dear William Burns was there. I can remember the first night it took place, on a Thursday night in August 1839. The good news spread over the city like fire, and every night, and sometimes in the morning, for many weeks, the church was crowded with seeking souls, and the young people came in great numbers. I was among them," she continues, "sitting at the foot of the pulpit stairs. It was then that the Spirit of God began His work of convincing me of sin. I can remember of weeping bitterly about my soul being lost, and I was often in the enquiry room, sometimes till one o'clock in the morning. Although I could not lay claim to any special text at that time as the means of my conversion, the Holy Spirit of God so drew me and showed me Jesus as the Saviour of sinners, and, blessed be His name, He has never left me from that day to this (say 4th December 1906), although I have often grieved Him. It is all due to free sovereign grace. Amen."

So you see Mr. M'Cheyne's prayers and William Burns' prayers were answered these days, and many gave their hearts to Jesus. It was when Ezekiel prayed, "Come from the four winds, O breath, and breathe upon these slain that they may live," that the dry bones stood up upon their feet an exceeding great army. We must go and do likewise. We must pray until the place is shaken. "In June 1861, a great assembly met on the South Inch of Perth. Rev. John Milne prayed, and it seemed as if the very ground were shaken at the presence of God." (The Rev. Duncan M'Gregor, Dundee.)

Mrs. Stewart, of Kinrossie, an old lady nearly ninety years of age, contributes the following nice bit about dear Mr. M'Cheyne. She is a very devoted and earnest Christian. Her mother lived until she was only five months short of the century. She remembers Mr. M'Cheyne very well, and as a girl was greatly struck with his intense earnestness in preaching. "While out walking, he seemed so completely absorbed in meditation that he passed people often and never saw them. When she was young she was serving in Dunsinnane House with the Nairns, and Mr. M'Cheyne was a guest there. His kindness of heart greatly struck her. He spoke so gently and sweetly to all the servants that she never forgot his kindness. In the pulpit he had not so much animation as spiritual power. What he said was from the heart, and it reached the heart of his hearers. The dominant influence of the district in which Mrs.

Stewart lives in Perthshire, amongst the old people,
is the fragrance of Dr. Andrew Bonar's ministry.   He
was indeed a noble and worthy companion and friend
of Mr. M'Cheyne, and truly in their case 'the memory
of the just is blessed' (Prov. x. 7).   I was requiring
some texts for our Soul-Winning and Prayer Union
several years ago, and as Dr. Bonar got our monthly
journal, *The Soul Winner*, at times, I asked him for a
few, when he replied as follows, and I write out the
full texts, and have prayed that God may bless
them :—

" 'GLASGOW, 20*th May* 1890.

" 'MY DEAR BROTHER,—I fear any texts I might
select may have been already appropriated.   Here
are three that I often, often use—

" 'ISAIAH lxi. 17-20.

" 'When the poor and needy seek water and there
is none, and their tongue faileth for thirst, I the Lord
will hear them, I the God of Israel will not forsake
them.

" 'I will open rivers in high places and fountains in
the midst of the valleys ; I will make the wilderness
a pool of water and the dry land springs of water.

" 'I will plant in the wilderness the cedar, the shittah
tree, and the myrtle and the oil tree ; I will set in
the desert the fir tree, and the pine and the box tree
together.

" 'That they may see, and know, and consider, and
understand together, that the hand of the Lord hath
done this, and the Holy one of Israel hath created it.'

" 'JEREMIAH xxxiii. 3.

" 'Call unto me, and I will answer thee, and shew

thee great and mighty things, which thou knowest not.'

"'JOB v. 8, 9.

"'I would seek unto God, and unto God would I commit my cause:

"'Which doeth great things and unsearchable; marvellous things without number.'—Yours truly in the Lord, (Signed) ANDREW A. BONAR."

Among the thatched cottages of Kinrossie, Miss Bonar writes in her nice book about her father, with its pretty village green and antique market cross, stands the Free Church of Collace.

Not far distant, on the edge of Dunsinnane wood, is the manse, hidden from view more than it was forty years ago by the growth of trees and hedges. A vine and a fig tree climb up on either side of the study window, and over other two windows are carved the Hebrew words, " He that winneth souls is wise," and "For yet a little while and He that shall come will come, and will not tarry." The path from the manse through Dunsinnane wood became a spot hallowed by prayer and communion with God. One day a man going along that way heard the sound of voices in the wood, and found Mr. Bonar kneeling there in prayer with two young men.

A young woman said to him—" I often wanted to die after I found Christ, for I was afraid of sinning; but one day I remembered Christ's words, ' I pray not that Thou shouldst take them out of the world, but that Thou shouldst keep them from the evil that is in the world,' and I don't want to die now."

I must still give a bit more from these beautiful pages of Miss Bonar's about her father and mother. Dr. Bonar's wife was brought to Christ during the revival in Edinburgh in 1842. She attended a prayer-meeting for the Jews in St. Andrew's Church, and Mr. M'Cheyne spoke, when the impression of his personal holiness rather than his words most deeply affected her. " There was something singularly attractive about him; it was not his matter nor his manner that struck me, it was just the living epistle of Christ—a picture so lovely I felt that I would have given all the world to be as he was, but knew all the time I was dead in sins." After she found the Saviour she dearly loved the 23rd Psalm, and long afterwards, when Dr. Bonar was dying, the words of that psalm sung beside his dying bed calmed the hearts of his children as they watched him passing to his Father's house on high.—See *Reminiscences of Dr. Andrew Bonar,* by his daughters.

When the revival broke out in St. Peter's Church, as narrated above by my friend, Miss Sime, Dundee, it was really a glorious time for us boys and girls, who had many meetings amongst ourselves, singing, praying, and calling on God.

Miss Sime continues her narrative as follows:— " The only meeting of boys and girls I remember of was in Isles Lane. There were a few of my school companions came with me; we met there for prayer before going to the church. One lad of the name of Tom Brown, who was brought up in the Orphan House in Small's Wynd, often led the meeting with great power in prayer, and so the work increased. After Mr. M'Cheyne returned to his flock from the Holy Land, there were more meetings of a private nature. My father was very zealous in the work, and he started one in our house on the Sabbath night after the Sabbath-school. I remember Mr. M'Cheyne visiting us one night, and he spoke a short time from Prov. ix. 13, to the end —a very solemn warning: "A foolish woman is clamorous — she is simple and knoweth nothing," etc. There were three or four of the girls who joined the church at the first Communion after he came home on 19th January 1840, at the age of twelve years. Then I myself joined at the next Communion in April of the same year. I was only between ten and eleven years old. What ups and downs since then! But I can truly say—'He has led me forth by the right way' (Ps. cvii. 7)."

I have already mentioned that I knew the lad here referred to above, who often led our boys' and girls' meeting with great power. And when Mr. M'Cheyne asked information about the children's meetings, he and I went to Mr. M'Cheyne's house with particulars. The servant let us in and took us to the kitchen, then went for the minister. He came in to where we were standing, but I cannot remember any more; perhaps the excitement had driven it from my mind.

Friends at a distance and in foreign lands might be pleased if I again refer to my early experiences in these glorious days of old. It was about the month of August 1839, when the great work began in Dundee, under Rev. William C. Burns, who was appointed to supply Mr. M'Cheyne's pulpit in St.

Peter's Church while he was absent in Palestine enquiring as to the state of the Jews. In answer to prayer, the Word of God came "in power, and in the Holy Ghost, and in much assurance" (1 Thess. i. 5). The hearts and consciences of the people were stirred to the very depths; the Word was quick and powerful, and large congregations filled the church nearly night after night, many being under deep concern about their souls' salvation. A large number of private meetings were also held; as many as thirty-nine were held weekly, and five of these were conducted by and attended entirely by children. At that time, by the grace and unmerited love of God, I was amongst the number who got the blessing. The spirit of prayer came down into our young hearts, and, praise the holy name of God, it is still burning brightly there at this day. The work of grace was deep, and spread to the neighbouring parishes—deep conviction of sin, and clear, gracious manifestations of the power of the Holy Ghost to the way of salvation, by believing and accepting the Lord Jesus as their Saviour from sin. At one time a drunkard finds the Saviour to be precious to his soul by believing. Another man describes his accepting the gift of God as by stooping and lifting up something at his feet. And the boys and girls of St. Peter's and district were graciously remembered by the Lord, and time after time we would meet to read the Scriptures and sing and pray together. Glorious, happy early days!

> "O blessed is the man to whom
> Is freely pardoned
> All the transgressions he hath done,
> Whose sin is covered." *Psalm* xxxii. 1.

And the Lord Jesus remains. And the throne of grace remains, and is often visited still, where we meet with God, and become endued with power from on high to love and serve our Divine Redeemer more and more. Oh, let us all be often there, to get the blessing from the Lord; then let us rise with the perfume of heaven about us to infect and bless others.

> "O that the world may taste and see
> The riches of His grace !
> The arms of love that compass me
> Would all mankind embrace."

Mr. M'Cheyne was very fond of the Song of Solomon (*Memoir and Remains*, pp. 480–482).

An able Eastern writer says, that in the East the people have a very pure and exquisite and lovely view of the marriage covenant, and of the love which brings to it.

And Mr. M'Cheyne said: "There is no book of the Bible which affords a better test of the depth of a man's Christianity than the Song of Solomon"; and as to some of its parts, notably chap. ii. vers. 8–17, he says: "He might well challenge the whole world of genius to produce in any language a poem such as this, so short, so comprehensive, so delicately beautiful. But what is far more to our purpose, there is no part of the Bible which shows up more beautifully some of the innermost experience of the believer's heart."—*Memoir and Remains*, pp. 480–482.

Mr. J. Small, Perth, encouraged me by writing at one time as follows: "Pray you may be guided to write what God will approve and greatly bless regarding His own wonderful working in 1839 and

1840 in Perth, as elsewhere in our highly-favoured land."

Such records are much calculated to awaken and quicken a spirit of importunate prayer, and to stimulate to greater Christian effort and expectation, that such outpourings of the Spirit may be graciously given again.

"We need a great revival, and increase of soul-saving work; and to have the Church purged from error, and worldliness, and clothed with new power from on high."

I received a communication from a Christian lady in Glasgow whose early days were much connected with thoughts of Mr. M'Cheyne, as her mother used his *Life and Sermons* as her constant subjects for reading.

I will add that this good seed has borne fruit in my friend and her family, whose good lives and work for the Master is well known to me and to the circle of their friends.

Just as a Christian gentleman, who used to come to have prayer with me, looked at me and solemnly said—" Ah! it's in the life."

So, reader, remember this wise saying of one now long been in the Better Land, " Ah! it's in the life."

The lady's note is as follows: " A daughter writes of her mother, now gone home, ' She loved M'Cheyne.'

"His *Life and Sermons* were her constant companions, and with her Bible and *The Christian*, almost her only books during her later years.

" The *Life* was her favourite gift to young men, and

at one time she sent Mr. Moody money to give a copy of it to each student in his Training Institute in Chicago.

"On one occasion a clergyman's wife asked my mother to pray for her son.

"My mother promised, adding, 'I shall pray that he may be a M'Cheyne.'"

I trust this prayer was answered for this young man.   God hears prayer.

XIV

OLD Thomas Watson, the Puritan, in his *Upright Man's Character*, says : " An upright Christian sets a crown of honour upon the head of religion ; he doth not only profess the Gospel, but adorns it; he labours to walk so regularly and holily that if we could suppose the Bible to be lost, it might be found again in his life."

We see in Robert Murray M'Cheyne a noble and beautiful life such as this, and I would humbly advise readers to procure a copy of Dr. Bonar's excellent memoir of this dear minister of Christ. In those days of agitation and amazing unrest, it would be a blessing to many and bring peace to their minds if they would study such gracious and true and noble lives like that of the sainted young minister of St. Peter's, Dundee.

Dr. Moody Stuart once wrote that it was a golden day when he first became acquainted with a young man so full of Christ as Robert M'Cheyne. And Dr. Andrew Bonar wrote of him : " There has been one among us who dwelt at the Mercy-seat as if it were his home ; preached the certainties of eternal life with an undoubting mind; and spent his nights and days in ceaseless breathings after holiness and the salvation of sinners. Hundreds of souls were his

reward from the Lord ere he left us, and in him have
we been taught how much one man may do who will
only press farther into the presence of his God, and
handle more skilfully the unsearchable riches of
Christ, and speak more boldly for his God."

My esteemed friend, the late Miss C. M. MacPhun,
of the Zenana Mission, Benares, India, presented me
with a copy of Dr. Bonar's *Reminiscences*, by his
daughter, which contains numerous notices of his
much-loved friend, Mr. M'Cheyne. The volume is
dated 30th October 1897. "Dear Andrew," he wrote,
"study to express yourself very clearly. I sometimes
observe obscurity of expression. Form your sentences
very regularly. It sometimes strikes me you begin
a sentence before you know where you are to end it,
or what is to come at the end."

The Kirkton of Collace is associated with the visits
of Robert M'Cheyne, who often rode over from
Dundee to give his services there. As he came to
the door one wintry day, he said : "I have been
riding all the way to-day through the pure white
snow, and that verse has been in my mind all the
time, 'Wash me, and I shall be whiter than snow'"
(Ps. li. 7). Mr. Bonar's old servant used to tell,
years afterwards, of Mr. M'Cheyne's last visit to
Collace. He preached in the church, and she told
how the people were standing out to the gate, and
the windows were pulled down that those outside
might hear. His text was, "Lest I myself should be
a castaway." She had to come away after he began,
and could see from the house the church lighted up,
and she wearied much for them to come home, but

the church was in that night till eleven o'clock.   The
people could not give over listening, and Mr. M'Cheyne
could not give over speaking.   She remembers the
time when Mr. Bonar could not get his tea taken for
the people coming and asking if conversion was true !
She greatly enjoyed hearing Mr. M'Cheyne at prayer
in the morning.   It was as if he could not give over,
he had so much to ask.   He used to rise at six on
Sabbath morning, and go to bed at twelve at night,
for he said he liked to have the whole day alone with
God.   At one time about sixty of the St. Peter's
people came from Dundee to the Collace Communion
in June 1843, after Mr. M'Cheyne had passed away.
The text was, " Until the day break and the shadows
flee away " (Song of Solomon iv. 6).   He referred to
Mr. M'Cheyne as standing on the "mountain of
myrrh" till the day break ; and as he pointed to the
bread and wine before him, as shadows that would
flee away, there came a great hush over the congregation, and then the sound of sobbing from the
Dundee people who were present, at the mention of
their beloved minister's name.   Mr. Bonar preached
at one time in St. Peter's upon the text, " Thine eyes
shall see the King in His beauty," when Mr. M'Cheyne
said, as they walked home together : " My brother,
you forgot there might be many listening to you
to-night who, unless they are changed by the grace
of God, shall never see Him in His beauty."   Dr.
Bonar, it is said, never afterwards preached a sermon
in which he did not commend Christ to the unsaved,
and rarely if ever closed without urging on his hearers
the immediate acceptance of the Saviour.—*Memoir.*

At one time Mr. M'Cheyne wrote a birthday ode
to his father, the two concluding lines of which are as
follow :—

> " We pray that, as oft as thy birthday appears,
> Thy purified joys may increase with thy years."

And now I continue these beautiful extracts from the
Reminiscences, with Dr. Bonar's words in an address
given to the children, that if their passions should
raise a storm, to remember Mr. M'Cheyne's verses :—

> " Peaceful and calm the tide of life,
>   When first I sailed with Thee ;
> My sins forgiven, no inward strife,
>   My breast a glassy sea.

> " But soon the storm of passion raves,
>   My soul is tempest-toss'd ;
> Corruptions rise, like angry waves :
>   ' Help, Master ! I am lost !'

> " ' Peace, peace, be still, thou raging breast,
>   My fulness is for thee ' :
> The Saviour speaks, and all is rest,
>   Like the waves of Galilee."—*Page* 332.

Mr. M'Cheyne visited Ireland twice, his visits being
much valued by his Presbyterian brethren. Many
were greatly stirred up by his preaching and by his
telling of the Lord's glorious work of grace in Scotland. His prayerfulness and consistent holiness left
their impressions on not a few, and it was during his
visit that a memorial was presented to the Irish
Assembly in behalf of a Mission to the Jews.

His little tract, "I love the Lord's Day," was

published 18th December 1841, but as convener of
the Sabbath Committee he had already written his
well-known letter to one of the chief defenders of the
Sabbath desecration.   " He continued unceasingly to
use every effort in this holy cause.   And is it not
worth the prayers and self-denying efforts of every
believing man?   Is not that day set apart as a season
wherein the Lord desires the refreshing rest of His
own love to be offered to a fallen world?"—*Memoir*,
p. 145.

In March 1842, Mr. Bonar and Mr. M'Cheyne
exchanged pulpits during several weeks, to enable
them to write their *Narrative of Mission to Israel
in Palestine*.   Often would Mr. M'Cheyne wander in
the mornings among the pleasant woods of Dunsinnane
Collace, till he had drunk in refreshment to his soul
by meditation on the Word of God, and then he
would take up his pen.   To a minister who inter-
rupted him he wrote: "You know, you stole away
my day, yet I trust all was not lost.   I think I have
had more grace ever since that prayer-meeting among
the fir-trees.   'Oh to be like Jesus, and with Him to
all eternity!'"   The *Narrative* was finished in May,
and the Lord has made it acceptable to the brethren.
I consider it a most excellent book, and have read in
it now and again with profit for many years.

When he returned to Dundee he writes:—" I have
seen some very evident awakenings of late.   J. G.,
awakened partly through the Word preached, and
partly through the faithful warnings of her fellow-
servant, M. B., converted last winter at the Tuesday
meeting in Annfield.   She was brought very rapidly

to peace with God, and to a calm, sedate, prayerful state of mind. I was surprised at the quickness of the work in this case, and pleased with the clear tokens of grace, and now I see God's gracious end in it. She was to be admitted at last Communion, but canght fever before the Sabbath. On Tuesday last she died in great peace and joy. When she felt death coming on she said, 'O death, death, come let us sing!' Many that knew her have been a great deal moved homeward by this solemn providence. I feel persuaded that if I could follow the Lord more fully myself, my ministry would be used to make a deeper impression than it has yet done."

On Mr. M'Cheyne's return from the Holy Land on 23rd November 1839, his assistant, Rev. W. C. Burns, closed his official connection with St. Peter's Church, Dundee. The following extracts will show his feelings and the tender bond of sacred affection which, in parting, bound him alike to that people and their pastor. Mr. Burns writes :—

"Had a letter from dear Mr. M'Cheyne, written in a spirit of joy for the work of the Lord.

"*Sabbath, November 17th,* 1839.—Just as I was concluding, it came into my mind that though I might probably preach to the people again, yet that now I had reached the termination of my ministry, and this gave me an affecting topic from which to press home the message more urgently, 'Union to Christ' (John xv.). The season was indeed one that I shall never forget. Before me there was a crowd of immortal souls, all hastening to eternity—some to heaven, and many, I fear, to hell—and I was called to speak to

them, as it were, for the last time, to press Jesus on
them, and to beseech them to be reconciled to God
by the death of His Son. After I had intimated that
Mr. M'Cheyne was expected to be here on Thursday,
I spoke a few words on my leaving them, but I was
so much affected that I could say but little. The
people retired very slowly when we had dismissed,
about five o'clock, and many waited in the passage
and in the gallery until I retired, who wept much
when I was passing along, and obliged me to pray
with them in the passage again. When I came out,
I met with many of the same affecting tokens of the
reality of my approaching separation from a people
among whom the Lord, in His sovereign and infinite
mercy, has shown me the most marvellous proofs of
His covenant love, and from among whom, I trust,
He has taken during my continuance among them
not a few jewels to shine for ever in the crown of
Emmanuel the Redeemer. Glory to the Lamb that
was slain!

"*November* 18*th.*—Truly the work of the Lord is
marvellous when I begin to look back upon it from
the beginning. It must engage my harp and my
tongue, with those of countless multitudes of the
redeemed in glory, throughout the endless ages of
eternity.

"*Friday, November* 24*th.*—I got safely home at
four o'clock from Dunfermline, and, after dining with
Mr. Thoms at five, I met Mr. M'Cheyne at his own
house at half-past six, and had a sweet season of
prayer with him before the hour of the evening
meeting. We went back into the pulpit, and after

we had sung and prayed shortly, I conducted the
remaining services, speaking from 2 Sam. xxiii.
2-5, and concluding at ten. We went to his house
together, and communed a considerable time about
many things connected with the work of God and his
and my own plans and prospects. I find he preached
to a densely crowded audience on Thursday night,
and with a deep impression, from 'I determined not
to know anything among you save Jesus Christ and
Him crucified' (1 Cor. ii. 2). He seems but in weak
health, and not very sanguine about ever resuming
the full duties of a parish minister. O Lord, spare
Thy servant, if it be for the glory of Thy name, and
restore his full strength, that he may yet be the means
of winning many souls for Jesus. Amen."

One evening, when the Rev. William C. Burns was
preaching in St. Peter's, the late Provost Moncur of
Dundee and I went along to hear him when we
were boys. Mr. Burns was quite of a different cast
of mind from Mr. M'Cheyne. The latter was tender
and holy and good. Of Mr. Burns it has been said:
"Gifted with a solid and vigorous understanding,
possessed of a voice of vast compass and power, and
withal fired with an ardour so intense and an energy
so exhaustless that nothing could damp or resist it,
Mr. Burns wielded an influence over the masses whom
he addressed which was almost without parallel since
the days of Wesley and Whitfield."

Crowds flocked to St. Peter's from all the country
round, and the strength of the preacher seemed to
grow with the incessant demands made upon it.
You might think him extreme—many did—but you

could not look at him without feeling—how truly!—
what a brilliant writer has said of John the Baptist,
applied to him — "He was homeless upon earth.
Well, but beyond—beyond—in the blue eternities
above—there was the prophet's home. He had cut
himself off from the solaces of life, but he was passing
into that country where it matters little whether a
man has been clothed in finest linen or in coarsest
camel's hair. Speech falls from him—sharp, rugged,
cutting. Repent. Wrath to come. The axe is laid
at the root of the tree. The fruitless trees will be
cast into the fire. He spoke as men speak when they
are in earnest, simply and abruptly, as if the graces
of oratory were out of place. And then that life of
his. There was written on it in letters that needed
no magnifying glass to read, 'Not of this world.'"
(Rev. Duncan Macgregor.)

We two boys heard the great preacher. Perhaps
my companion, A. H. Moncur, got a rich spiritual
blessing that night, for very few men have set such a
wise, and good, and holy example around them as
he did even from early years. He was an elder of
the M'Cheyne Memorial Church, Dundee, a member
of our consecrated Pen Circle—to use our pens for
Jesus; and a firm temperance reformer, as we all
know. He seemed to have a kindly instinct,
earnestly to be ready for the call, wherever was to be
found suffering, distress, or need.

> "Thus to relieve the wretched was his pride,
> And even his failings leaned to virtue's side."

It was Miss Havergal who said "she wished to

crowd into her life all she could possibly do for Jesus," and so it is to Him we have to give our hearts; it is to Him we have to give our silver and our gold; it is to our dear Redeemer who died for us, to whom we should give ourselves, our daily labour, and our earnest love; and it will be a serious thing for you, reader, if at the last you find that you never cut a sheaf in the harvest of the Lord.

On one occasion, before a large audience in Dundee, the Rev. John M'Neill, the preacher, looked round the church, and said he might call for testimony to the reality of the Christian hope from many in that assembly, but he would just ask his friend Provost Moncur to say a word. Many of the audience, knowing his reticence in this direction, were afraid he would not answer, but he stood to his feet, and, amidst breathless silence, testified that for long years now the peace of God had possessed his heart—that he stood in the light of God that night, for his faith was resting on the finished work of Jesus Christ our Saviour.

A friend who served on his teaching staff in the Sabbath-school for a quarter of a century wrote:—
" I had frequent occasions to mark his quiet but deep evangelical fervour. Many a time have I seen his eye kindle as he repeated the lines—

> " ' I asked them whence their victory came?
> They with united breath
> Ascribed the glory to the Lamb,
> Their triumph to His death.' "

I had my last serious conversation with Provost

Moncur on 20th October 1902. We spoke of having played together in our young days, and having prayed together in the days of M'Cheyne. I said, " But we are going to hold to the righteousness and atoning blood of Christ." " O yes," he replied, " that's the foundation." " Well," I said, " I am to hold to that by grace to the end, and you too." " O yes," he answered. " Well, let us hold to the foundation to the last, for I am solemnly impressed that we are getting up in years and have to look to it." " O yes," he again replied, " that's the way." And now, behold, our good early friend and brother in the Lord has left us, and entered into the eternal rest that remaineth for the people of God.

"It is not death to fling
        Aside this sinful dust,
    And rise on strong exulting wing,
        To live among the just.

"Jesus ! Thou Prince of life !
        Thy chosen cannot die ;
    Like Thee, they conquer in the strife,
        To reign with Thee on high."

But I would like to tell about another dear elder of the church, who was ordained at the same time as myself, in April 1856, by our dear pastor, the Rev. Charles Nairn, of Free St. David's, Dundee.

This was Mr. Alexander Blackie, with whom I had much happy Christian fellowship for a number of years.

A stern temperance reformer, and an earnest labourer in the vineyard of the Lord, and latterly an elder also in the M'Cheyne Memorial Church, Dundee.

Then he and his family went to Chicago, where I had the pleasure of visiting them.

But now we must bid them good-bye, and we meet in their home to have a parting season of prayer. We read the Word of God, and then joined in singing the 2nd Paraphrase, which we have been accustomed to do since our early days, and our prayers then ascend to our God and Father in Christ Jesus :—

"O God of Bethel! by whose hand
Thy people still are fed;
Who through this weary pilgrimage
Hast all our fathers led.

"Our vows, our prayers, we now present
Before Thy throne of grace;
God of our fathers! be the God
Of their succeeding race.

"Through each perplexing path of life
Their wand'ring footsteps guide;
Give us each day our daily bread,
And raiment fit provide.

"O spread Thy cov'ring wings around,
Till all our wand'rings cease,
And at our Father's loved abode
Our souls arrive in peace.

"Such blessings from Thy gracious hand
Our humble prayers implore;
And Thou shalt be our chosen God,
And portion evermore."

By and by, we arrived home in Scotland. Another by and by passed over us, when behold the sad news was received by us that our dear old friend and fellow-worker for Christ had passed away into eternity, to be for ever with the Lord. "The Lord gave, and the Lord hath taken away; blessed be the name of the Lord."   Amen.

Lord, may I like the valiant soldier fall,
One of the storming party on the wall,
Ever to Jesus and His Word be true,
Ever with heaven and "Well done" in my view.

Give me the new, clean heart that loves the Lord,
The Holy Spirit-filled life, taught by Thy Word,
Thy glory still advanced while on life's road,
A joyful entrance through death's gates to God.

XV.

ONE day in the pulpit Mr. M'Cheyne said— "Here is a Bible; it just cost a shilling, but there is as much in it as has saved my soul."

An old lady friend of mine, Mrs. Smith from Methven, Perthshire, heard him say this, and saw him holding up the Bible, and she thinks it was at a Thursday night's meeting, when he was asking all his people to get Bibles and read them. Mr. M'Cheyne asked her if she had one. She said "No." He then gave her one, and she has it yet. She heard him preach the sermon, "Be diligent," when he said—"Ah! you that are unconverted, you never think of these things. But we (believers) are like a man who lives in a crazy house; we long to go away."

In his conversation with this lady, in his own house, he said—"Have you been a great sinner?" She could not speak in reply. He then told dear old Mr. John Mathewson, the elder, that he often saw the tear trickling down her cheek. What gave her peace was a little book by Rev. Horatius Bonar, named *Believe and Live*, which said, "Whenever we believed in Christ, all our sins were taken away." "And I took Him, and hid under His wing, and

trusted Him, and He has given me glorious times
with Himself." "There have been dark clouds, but
He has kept me in deep peace—a deep peace, a
grand peace, that the world could not touch, and
sometimes a blessed joy."

My friend, by and by, was able to speak to anxious
souls. "At one time, when Richard Weaver and
Radcliffe were here," she said, "I was asked to go
and speak to a soul; but, O dear me! could I speak
to an anxious soul? I went home, rather, and I
opened the Bible at these words, Jer. xxvi. 2,
'Stand and speak and diminish not a word.' I went
off to the meeting; it was near midnight, and I
spoke to the women there. I was able to speak to
many, and they would sit down on a form, and just
a word or two would help them. In Carrubber's
Close, a young man said that it would take a month
for Jesus to save him. But I got him on his knees
and prayed; then he prayed himself; rose up and
believed there and then, and said, 'I'm saved.' That
laddie wrote me three months afterwards that he was
very glad he had taken Jesus to be His Saviour that
night, for he was quite happy, and found it was the
happiest life, and..he was now working for the
Lord."

After reading the above simple narrative, the
reader may frankly admit that the question has been
fairly answered, "What's the good of being religious?"
Much peace, and comfort, and blessing, and power,
has been the possession of my dear aged friend who
visited me that day some time ago, and told me her
lovely, artless tale. Year by year the Lord has been

her keeper, and will be, even unto the end, so she can say with the sweet singer of old:

> "And I will constantly go on
>   In strength of God the Lord,
> And thine own righteousness, even Thine
>   Alone, I will record."
>
> *Psalm* lxxi. 16.

Another very nice verse in the 11th Paraphrase may be a help to any one who may be wondering if there is any use being a Christian : what advantage would there be in embracing the celestial wisdom offered without money and without price?   Answer—

> "Her ways are ways of pleasantness,
>   And all her paths are peace."

Mr. M'Cheyne visited James Talbert, who was so many years an invalid, living at first (when I used to see him) in a lonely cottage on the Camperdown estate, west a little from Lochee; but who was spared to be the helper and comforter of many who visited him, for the long period of over sixty years.   His old nurse thinks that the Rev. Andrew Bonar was with Mr. M'Cheyne at that visit, and James told her what a solemn, serene countenance the young minister of St. Peter's had, with a heavenly expression, and he was so quiet.   Mr. M'Cheyne spoke to James from the 84th Psalm, especially verse sixth — "Who, passing through the valley of Baca, make it a well; the rain also filleth the pools."

Mr. M'Cheyne did not consider it right to decide the path of duty by signs and tokens.   He believed

that the written Word supplied sufficient data for
guiding the believing soul, and when certain pro-
vidential occurrences happened, he regarded them as
important only so far as they might be answers to
prayer.   Indeed, he himself has left us a glance of
his views on this point, in his verses, which may have,
as a fragment, been written about this time on
" Gideon's Fleece ":—

> "When God called Gideon forth to fight,
> 'Go, save thou Israel in thy might;'
> The faithful warrior sought a sign
> That God would on his labours shine.
> But when the message which we bring
> Is one to make the dumb man sing,
> To bid the blind man wash and see,
> The lame to leap with ecstasy,
> To raise the soul that's bowed down,
> To wipe away the tears and frown,
> To sprinkle all the heart within
> From the accusing voice of sin,
> Then such a sign my call to prove,
> To preach my Saviour's dying love,
> I cannot, dare not, hope to find."

Also, he did not consider that if churches were
built and ministers endowed, this would of itself be
sufficient to reclaim the multitudes of perishing men.
But he sought and expected that the Lord would
send faithful men into His vineyard.   New churches
were to be like cisterns, ready to catch the shower
when it should fall, just as his own new church did
in the day of the Lord's power.   His views on this
subject were summed up in the following lines,
written one day as he sat in company with some of

his earnest brother ministers, who were deeply anxious
for church extension over the land :—

> "Give me a man of God, the Truth to preach,
> A house of prayer within convenient reach,
> Seat rents the poorest of the poor can pay,
> A spot so small one pastor can survey :
> Give these, and give the Spirit's genial shower,
> Scotland shall be a garden all in flower."

There was in Mr. M'Cheyne's character a high
refinement that came out in poetry and true polite-
ness, and there was something in his graces that
reminded one of his own remarks.   At one time he
was speaking from the Song of Solomon, iv. 16 :
" Awake, O north wind ; and come, thou south, blow
upon my garden, that the spices thereof may flow
out," which the title to the chapter explains, namely,
Christ setteth forth the graces of the Church.   He
showeth His love to her.   The Church prayeth to be
made fit for His presence.   Mr. M'Cheyne said :
" Some believers were a garden that had fruit trees,
and so were useful ; but we ought also to have spices,
and to be attractive."   I personally consider these
remarks to be most beautiful, and to a minister
most necessary and important.   The apostle gives a
fine exposition of the thought in Phil. iv. 8, 9 :
" Finally, brethren, whatsoever things are true, whatsoever things are honest, whatsoever things are just,
whatsoever things are pure, whatsoever things are
lovely, whatsoever things are of good report, if there
be any virtue, and if there be any praise, think on
these things."   " Those things which ye have both
learned and received, and heard and seen in Me, do ;

and the God of peace shall be with you." The above
high attainments Mr. M'Cheyne seemed to press
forward to, and thus, as a minister, was always able
to set a wise and good and holy example around
him, most important for us all, as professing followers
of our Lord and Saviour, Jesus Christ; but in a
minister *absolutely necessary*, or his light may simply
be darkness.

Wishing to convey his grateful feelings to a fellow-
minister in Dundee, Mr. M'Cheyne sent him a Hebrew
Bible, with these few lines :—

> " Anoint mine eyes,
>   O Holy dove !
> That I may prize
>   This Book of Love.
>
> " Unstop mine ear
>   Made deaf by sin,
> That I may hear
>   Thy voice within.
>
> " Break my hard heart,
>   Jesus, my Lord ;
> In the inmost part
>   Hide Thy sweet word."

Mr. M'Cheyne's absorbing love for the Jews is very
well known, and in his interesting narrative of his
mission to them in Palestine, I have often read.
When Scotland commenced its mission to the Jews,
the very first convert to Christianity was the late
Adolph Saphir, who became a very eminent minister
of the gospel, and wrote several excellent books in
favour of the Scriptures, which, by the grace of God,

had made him "wise unto salvation, through faith, which is in Christ Jesus" (2 Tim. iii. 15). I have several of his volumes, very useful at the present time, when the enemy has come in like a flood, and they are crucifying the Lord afresh and putting Him to an open shame. This interesting mission seemed to be an answer to the prayers of a good man in Glasgow, Mr. Woodrow.

He kept on, sometimes fasting and pleading with God for a whole day, that Israel might be forgiven and restored. And so in 1837 a memorial was presented to the General Assembly, and a mission was established in Palestine. Then one day Dr. Candlish and Dr. Moody Stuart, while standing in a street in Edinburgh considering the weak health of their young friend, Robert M'Cheyne, all of a sudden Dr. Candlish said, "What do you think of sending Mr. M'Cheyne to Palestine, to inquire into the state of the Jews?" This led to the formation of the deputation—Dr. Keith, Dr. Black, Mr. M'Cheyne, and his dear friend Andrew Bonar, and in due time they went off to the Holy Land, with great results unto the lost sheep of the house of Israel. My friend Mr. W. J. Lockie, London, secretary to the Paris City Mission, writes me:—"I am much interested in the articles about the saintly M'Cheyne and revivals. This lovely couplet was composed by him, profound in thought, and so true:—

> "'We are spirits clothed in veils,
>   man by man was never seen;
> All our deep communion fails
>   to remove the shadowy screen.'"

I have already shown in these articles how readily
he could express himself in chaste and beautiful
verses of hymns or poems, and I mention on page
111 the sad case of a lady, a friend of the M'Cheyne
family, who had said "that she was determined to
keep by the world," and quote the lines which Mr.
M'Cheyne wrote on her melancholy decision.   In an
address to a Y.M.C.A. Bible-class the late Rev. Dr.
Andrew Bonar referred to these lines, and to the circumstances attending their composition.   Dr. Bonar
said: "Shortly after his conversion, M'Cheyne wrote
a piece of poetry to a young lady who was very gay.
The lady read it, smiled, and laid it in her desk.
One year, at one of the meetings of the Mildmay
Conference, a lady came up to me, asked me to speak
with her, and said: 'I was a great friend of one who
was a great friend of yours, Robert M'Cheyne.   I am
the lady to whom he wrote the poem.   When I heard
of his death I remembered the verses.   I searched for
them, read them over, and was awakened and converted.'   I asked if she still had them, and if I might
see them, to which she kindly agreed.   'But,' she
said, 'return them, for I will never part with the
arrow that reached my heart.'   So, you see, many
years after the lines were written they were used.
Sow seed, and let God make it spring up when He
sees best."

I am able to take up the tale of these lines where
Dr. Bonar leaves it.   Some time ago, when the articles
that form the basis of this book were appearing in a
Scottish temperance magazine, I received an interesting letter from my esteemed friend, Mrs. J. Macleish,

Aberfeldy, as follows:—"Many thanks for *Scottish Reformer*, with your account of revival times in Dundee, under M'Cheyne, etc. In the one I got last week (9th November 1906), there were the lines to a young lady who said 'she had chosen the world.' As you did not mention the incident, you may not have heard that these lines were the means of her conversion. She died some years ago, and when her friends were looking over some of her boxes, they found a sheet of paper with these lines written out, carefully kept. An account of it was published in some magazine, but I forget which, so in case you may not have heard this, I could not help writing to tell you. I heard an English Church clergyman telling us at the Perth Conference, about fifteen or sixteen years ago, that he was proud to be on the same platform with Dr. Andrew Bonar, the writer of M'Cheyne's *Memoir*, and that not a day passed without his reading part of that book. These articles you are publishing in that paper are bound to be a blessing; they are so refreshing to those of us who have often read them, and must be a treat to any who have not read them before."

It is stated that Mr. M'Cheyne said, " Live so as to be missed," which will be admitted to be very good advice, for we should not be dark clouds, or the subject of aversion or scorn by all around. No, let our light shine in our homes, and in our daily life and duty, as sunbeams. Let us commend our Lord and Master whom we serve, to all, by our honest dealing and lovely lives, and let us seek to please our Heavenly Father, "to be approved of

God, and have our name recorded in the book of
Life" (Pollock).

> A sunbeam burst out
>   From the clouds on a day,
> And soon drove the darkness
>   And mists all away.
>
> So may I beam out, Lord,
>   With love and with power,
> And be a bright sunbeam
>   For Thee from this hour.

I must now conclude this section with a most
interesting communication which I have received
from my late dear aged friend, Mrs. W. Nairn, sen.,
of Dundee, she having been a convert under Mr.
M'Cheyne in these glorious revival days:—" Many
thanks for your kindness in sending me the paper
about dear Mr. M'Cheyne. It brought back the
memory of many a precious walk and conversation I
had with him. I was one of the two you mention
whom he admitted as church members under eleven
years of age. He was anxious I should join the
church, but Mr. Reid thought I was too young. Mr.
M'Cheyne said 'if I was not too young to be in
Christ, I was not too young to be at His table.' He
was a great believer in prayer. I remember him
coming to me after the prayer-meeting, and asking
me if I would come and see him about seven in the
morning, as he had to go with the ten o'clock train,
and I will never forget the hour we spent together in
prayer and conversation. Then he wrote Mr. Reid
a letter on his knees. He told me to take everything
to Jesus, however small, just as I did to him, for He

is not only able to help you, but He loves to have
communion and fellowship with those He loves. I
remember going to meet him at Auldbar station, as
he was going to preach on the Thanksgiving Monday,
so that I would have three miles to walk with him.
He spoke to every man and woman we met so
lovingly and to the point. One woman was herding
a sheep and a cow, and he asked her if they were
hers, then he said, 'Do you know the great Shepherd
of the sheep?' I can never forget the sermon he
preached that Monday. He brought you to feel you
were a lost sinner, and he pictured the realities of
eternity so vividly before you. I was thought dying
the last Sabbath he preached, and the doctors told
my father (the late good old Mr. John Mathewson)
there was no hope, so he went to the church that
afternoon and told Mr. M'Cheyne, who then asked
prayer for me in the church; and when my father
came home there was a change for the better, so I
was the last one he prayed for in public. His simple
faith in prayer, in telling Jesus everything, has been
a great comfort to me when I was left a widow with
eight children; but the Lord has been to me all He
promised, and more than all I thought He would
have been. Oh! what deliverances He has wrought
for me, and how many wonderful answers to prayer,
often neither at the time nor in the way I expected,
but in His own way and at His own time. One
year, when attending the Keswick Convention, Mr.
C. A. Fox was closing one of the meetings with
prayer and the singing of a hymn. When this was
done, he stood up and said: 'I feel there is some

one here who has not cast their burden on the Lord,
and I have asked Him to guide me in prayer.'   Then
he prayed for fathers and mothers, sisters and brothers.
After a pause he said again: 'Is there a widow here
who can trust the Lord with her sons who are at
home, but not with those who are away from home;
she cannot trust the Lord wholly!'   This was my
very case.   During that prayer I was enabled to give
over the three absent ones to Him, and He brought
two of them to Himself shortly after that.   I am still
waiting on Him for the third.   You have often had
his case in the *Soul Winner*.   Please remember him
still that we may be an unbroken circle in heaven—a
whole family saved, not one awanting.   It was very
cheering to me when my son told me you were praying for me.   I suffer a great deal of pain and get but
little sleep at nights, but He says, 'Fear not, for I am
with thee.'   It is many years now since He said to
me, 'I will never leave thee; I will never forsake
thee,' and now when I am old, and need Him more
than ever, He will not forsake me.   I often think of
that grand gallery of faith in the eleventh of Hebrews.
What courage and endurance they showed, and how
they were lifted above their circumstances and enabled
to look forward to Him whom they saw only afar
off; but we look back now and see Him who not
only died but rose again for us.   How ashamed I am
of my little faith and confidence in Him, who has
done so much for me and mine.   Please pray that I
may have the strength and patience I need to do His
blessed will.   I often think of you and your grand
work.   May the Lord strengthen you more and

more, is the prayer of your friend in Christ Jesus,—
E. NAIRN."

My dear friend Mrs. James Scrymgeour of Newport has told me numbers of stories of the olden
time, and the following are connected with the days
of M'Cheyne.   Her husband, of whom we write with
the deepest respect and love, laboured late and early
in the good cause of temperance and godliness, and
would tell her how he would see Mr. M'Cheyne
in these early days, and take notice of the dear
minister whose very appearance deeply impressed
him.

An old woman who used to be about, would also
tell her of the meetings in St. Peter's Church, and
say, "Oh, what a grand meeting we had!"   Another
would say, "Oh, the times we had, coming from the
Church of St. Peter's, singing hymns!" meaning, I
suppose, in these early days of M'Cheyne in
Dundee.

The day Mr. M'Cheyne died this same lady had
a little sister who also died; so she came along and
said, "Mr. M'Cheyne and my little sister have entered
glory to-day."   Another old lady used to go along
to the grave and kneel down—which was a rather
startling sight, as she would be frequently seen on
her knees where the dear minister lay.

I cannot pass this point until I mention in loving
terms one of M'Cheyne's successors, the Rev. Duncan
M'Gregor.

He was a man I greatly esteemed, although he cost
me many a tear when I at times sat in St. Peter's
Church hearing him preach.

One day I visited his church, when he seemed to be addressing a large Bible-class.

By and by he noticed me, and called me up to the platform below the pulpit, and after a time called for me to pray.

I consider that it was a great honour to pray for these dear young people in the church of Robert Murray M'Cheyne.

Again I visited the church when Mr. M'Gregor was speaking on the text, Eph. i. 3, "Heavenly places in Christ."

He thought the Lord had chosen some countries more than others, some towns more than others, to be blessed by the Gospel. Then for ourselves, some houses more blessed to us than others, some rooms in the house more than others, some corners of the room where we may have given our hearts to Jesus.

So, reader, do you recollect the place where you gave your heart to Jesus?

Mr. Thomas Leith, of Edinburgh, has a kindly word as follows :—" Many thanks for sketch of Mr. M'Cheyne (Chap. XX.), which I now return. I well remember the funeral, and services in St. Peter's following Sabbath, which I attended, hearing Mr. Somerville and Mr. Bonar. At the funeral I stood opposite gate entrance to burying ground.

"There will be some wonderful rehearsal of the ways by which God has led us, as in the life eternal we meet those whom we have loved and known, and with whom we have had sweet fellowship. Grace, mercy, and peace be with you.—Yours, as ever, in Christ Jesus, THOMAS LEITH."

Then come some interesting suggestions from a good friend in Broughty Ferry, Mr. James Watt. First, " That a meeting might be convened of all in the district who have in any way been benefited by reading Mr. M'Cheyne's memoirs or sermons." I am not able for this at my age and with my present health, but will be very pleased to hear from any one on the subject. Second suggestion, " That my articles should be published in a book." " I am sure," he adds, " it would have a good circulation."

Here is a good and very practical word from Mr. J. Yule, who gave me the hint lately that Mr. M'Cheyne's manse was to be pulled down (see engraving, Chap. XXI.):—" Thanks very much for the perusal of your article on revivals in Dundee. May the Lord bless it in stimulating the faith of all under whose eyes it falls. We cannot but feel sure that the locality with such sacred memories will yet be visited in a manner even more marked by the Spirit when He lifts up a standard against the enemy, and makes the ' dry bones ' live.

" How true to fact is the remark of Rev. A. Bonar, ' that the world will stand the hottest fire at pulpit distances, if preachers only accommodate themselves on other occasions.'

" May God save us from professionalism, and give us, each true believer, more realism.—Yours in the faith, J. YULE."

Another friend writes :—" I read M'Cheyne's book yet; it's just like the Bible, always fresh."—MISS FERGUSON, Crieff."

Some relics of Mr. M'Cheyne are still in existence. If any friend has an interesting relic, it might be sent to Rev. Andrew Moody, D.D., 69 Merchiston Crescent, Edinburgh, for the museum in that city.

XVI

BUT what is a revival? It is a return to life and activity and vigour in our Christian walk and work and experience. It is to be quickened and renewed and restored, after we may have fallen away from our first love to Jesus Christ, our dear Redeemer, who died for us.

In these moments or times of revival, when the blessed Holy Spirit draws near to the people of God in power and in love, our hearts are lifted above the world, our souls pant after God, the living God, and much of our time is spent in adoring and admiring the bleeding Lamb, who died on Calvary. The believer in these times of revival begins again. He gets up a step, and goes from faith to faith, from strength to strength, from profession to reality, from twilight gloom to the morning of peace and joy.

> "And when he tastes his Saviour's love,
>   And feels the rapture strong;
> Scarce the divinest harp above
>   Aims at a sweeter song."

One of the first things we may do when a revival of religion begins amongst us, is to take the dusty Bible down from the shelf. It is to be a mere article of furniture no longer, although that would not be so bad as to be scorned and sneered at as now. Its blessed pages are bright with the light of truth and heaven. Its effect upon the heart is now marvellous; as the Holy Ghost, its author, shines upon its blessed words of love.

> " A glory gilds the sacred page,
>   Majestic, like the sun;
> It gives a light to every age—
>   It gives, but borrows none."

The believer's revived life is an inspiration to those in his family circle, in his business or ministry, and to all around; even the heathen feel and participate in the waves of heavenly power, as his prayers and his means float along to their distant shores. I am old enough to have seen and felt these happy days.

> A time of blessing on our country dawned,
> The Word was preached with power throughout the land;
> Conversions (now believed in) came with power,
> And crowds accepted Jesus hour by hour.

Children and young people are not beneath the attention and the influences of the Divine Spirit in these days. I remember the revival in M'Cheyne's days quite well. The work of grace was great, and spread to the neighbouring parishes, with deep conviction of sin, and in numberless cases clear, gracious manifestations of the way of salvation through faith in a crucified Redeemer. The old people held many private prayer-meetings in the town; as many as thirty-nine were held weekly. The boys and girls were not overlooked, and the spirit of prayer was poured into our young hearts, so that five meetings were attended by and entirely conducted by us young people in those bright and happy days. Time after time we would meet together to sing and pray and read the Scriptures, which we believed and loved from board to board with implicit faith and confidence. Several of the young folks of these early days are still to the fore, and are known to me.

Just lately I visited and prayed with an old lady in Newport, Mrs. Wanless, who joined Mr. M'Cheyne's church about sixty-seven years ago. There were thirty-two communicants at the same time, and she was between fourteen and fifteen years of age. That was the time when the two young girls under fourteen years were admitted to the Lord's Supper.

Two young boys, James Laing and James Wallace, were admitted at that time also, both of whom were made the subjects of interesting papers by Mr. M'Cheyne and Mr. W. C. Burns. "Another Lily Gathered," written by M'Cheyne, is the beautiful story of Jamie Laing, as he was called, and might be profitably read at the present time to show the lovely work of grace and the early call to glory in this young boy.

She said—"Mr. M'Cheyne took them into the vestry one by one from the class-room, as they were applying to be young communicants. 'What is your reason for thinking of coming to the Lord's table, Mary?' he asked. She replied, 'Jesus says, If you love Me, keep My commandments, and I

love Jesus.'   Mr. M'Cheyne then said, 'A very
good reason, Mary.'   She and another girl, who
were both neglected orphans, were greatly cared for
by him, and he would come down from the pulpit
on Thursday night after the prayer-meeting, and
say, 'I'll have an evening to spend with you and
Jessie Chephen.'   Then when we went into his
house he would sit down and take the Bible and
make us read verse about, and explained it to us,
and the last time he read to us the verses, Eph.
v. 1, 2: 'Be ye therefore followers of God, as dear
children.   And walk in love, as Christ also hath
loved us, and hath given Himself for us, an offering
and a sacrifice to God for a sweet smelling savour.'
Then he made us both kneel down with him in
prayer.   He would say, 'Pray you first, Mary, and
I will pray after you,' and then whatever was our
requests he would perhaps pray it in different words.
We were often in his house, and I was engaged to
be an assistant servant to him when he died.   When
I called at the house in the evening, he would say
to his housekeeper, 'Glenny, give Mary some
supper, and bring her in to the worship.'

    "In 1841 there was great stagnation of trade in
Dundee.   I was in trouble, and was out of employment, and was without food; but one day 1 found
a sixpence, and lived a week on it.   Then one day,
as we were returning from a meeting in Invergowrie,
Mr. M'Cheyne came behind me, and said, 'I hear
you are out of employment, Mary; take this.'   And
he offered me four shillings, but I refused it, when
he said, 'You are a very bad-mannered girl, Mary;

if you will not take it from me, take it from Christ, as we are Christ's stewards.'"

As the dull trade continued, she thought of going to work in France. When Mr. M'Cheyne heard of it, he said, " I am afraid for your soul, Mary, for France is a very wicked place. I will take you for a second servant." " I was to go to him at the May term in 1842, but he died on the 24th March, while I was visiting an aunt in Montrose. But I came to the funeral, and oh! it was a place of weeping."

" At my first communion," she said, " with Mr. M'Cheyne in St. Peter's, he preached, then served the Communion tables, then addressed the communicants, and said, as Hos. xiv. 8: 'What have I to do any more with idols?' He said he knew a young woman who was offered a garland of flowers, which she refused, saying, 'How could I wear flowers on my brow when Christ wore thorns.' When Mr. M'Cheyne had told this, the young women at the Communion table began to pull the flowers out of their bonnets and stamped them under their feet, and we never put a rose in our bonnets for years after that, only a ribbon. Then, proceeding, he called heaven and earth to witness, as he charged them all, wholly to be Christ's now and Christ's for ever. This was my first Communion, in October 1840, when thirty-two young people joined the Church at the same time; and by the next Communion two of these young communicants were dead, namely, Jamie Laing and a girl; and Mr. M'Cheyne said, 'There were two with us at last communion, and now they were sitting at the table above.'

"It was always impressive; Mr. M'Cheyne drew you. In old St. David's Church in Dundee one night he showed numerous things which he had brought from Palestine, and told of having knelt at Gethsemane, where Jesus Christ had knelt. He showed corn which he had brought from Jerusalem, and testified against any one who did not believe in the testimony of God against that city, 'Zion shall be ploughed like a field' (Jer. xxvi. 18)."

We see from the above interesting story, told me by my aged, afflicted friend in Newport, how kind a heart the young minister of St. Peter's had, how even two young, poor, neglected orphans were not beneath his notice and kind attentions, and how he took pains to instruct them and help them, and lead them to Jesus.

Truly "the memory of the just is blessed," and to think of these kind and loving ways of Mr. M'Cheyne should be as an inspiration to ministers and all to follow in his steps.

> "Go, bid the hungry orphan be
>   With thy abundance blest ;
> Invite the wanderer to thy gate,
>   And spread the couch of rest.
>
> "Let him who pines with piercing cold
>   By thee be warmed and clad ;
> Be thine the blissful task to make
>   The downcast mourner glad."
>
> *Paraphrase* xxviii.

I wish I could recall these features I have seen in his pulpit myself, and in his home, in these early days. The youthful minister, so good, so noble, so holy; but his own lines in trying to remember his brother David's countenance may give an idea of the difficulty in endeavouring to remember the exact shades and forms of our dear ones gone before :—

> "Alas! in vain; come hither, painter, come,
>   Take up once more thine instruments, thy brush
>   And palette, as thy haughty art be, as thou say'st,
>   Omnipotent, and if thy hand can dare
>   To wield creative power.   Renew thy toil,
>   And let my memory, vivified by love,
>   Which Death's cold separation has but warmed
>   And rendered sacred, dictate to thy skill
>   And guide thy pencil . . . of him,
>   Unwearied mining in the precious stores
>   Of classic lore; and better, nobler still,
>   In God's own Holy Writ."

But in Mr. M'Cheyne's *Memoir*, by Dr. Andrew Bonar, we have a beautiful mental likeness of him who is gone to his reward, which all may read with instruction, profit, and inspiration as follows :—

" Here is a word for doctors.   Writing to a medical friend, he says, ' I remember, long ago, a remark you once made, namely, that medical men ought to make a distinct study of the Bible, purely for the sake of administering conviction and consolation to their patients.'   I think this advice is very good and practical.   The first time I heard a doctor praying with a patient was, I think, as follows :—I held cottage meetings in an old man's house at one time when I was young, and I trust spoke for eternity. He took a violent fit of blood-vomiting one day in my presence.   The doctor was sent for, who prayed with him.   I was greatly impressed that a doctor

should pray with a patient.   The sickness continued,
and I frequently called.   Sometimes he would be in
great distress about his soul, crying out, 'Oh! can I
be saved?'   I read and prayed with him, and cried
to God for help, offering him Jesus as a Saviour for
his soul.   After a lingering illness he died, I trust,
looking to and resting on the Lamb of God, 'who
taketh away the sins of the world.'"

But many a time since then has my own doctor
and friend here, the late Dr. Stewart, prayed with me
for comfort and for peace.

Here is a word from Mr. M'Cheyne for ministers.
On hearing a very good sermon, but no earnest conclusion, he charged the speaker to warn those who
cared for none of these things, or made religion a
mere form, and were yet in their sins, or such like.

Here is a word to the bereaved :—" I earnestly trust
that this sad bereavement may be greatly blessed by
God to you.   Pray that you may not lose this
precious opportunity of giving your hand and heart
for ever away to the Lord Jesus.   How sweet that
Jesus ever liveth.   He is the same yesterday, and
to-day, and for ever.   He is like a rose blooming in
the midst of the desolation, a rock rising above the
storm.   The Bible, too, is more full of meaning.   Oh!
precious Book, that conveys such a message to the
mourner's dwelling, 'He doth not afflict willingly'
(Lev. iii. 33)."

Here is a solemn word to the young, to a young
invalid boy anxious about his soul: "If the Lord
Jesus would but draw the curtain and let you see His
own fair face and His wounded side, and how there

is room for the guiltiest sinner in Him, you would be drawn to Jesus by the cords of love. I was preaching in Perth last Sabbath. When I came out, a little girl came up to me, I think about three or four years old. She wanted to hear of the way to be saved. Her mother said she had been crying the whole night before about her soul, and would take no comfort till she should find Jesus. Oh! pray that the same Spirit may waken you. You once wept for your soul too, and prayed and sought Jesus. Have you found Him? or have you looked back? Awake again and call upon the name of the Lord. Your time may be short, God only knows. The longest lifetime is short enough. It is all that is given you to be converted in. They are the happiest who are brought soonest to the bosom of Jesus. May you all meet at the table of Jesus above, and may I be there too, a sinner saved by grace." This dear boy died a few weeks after this letter was written.—*Memoir and Remains.*

Mr. M'Cheyne's biographer, the Rev. Andrew Bonar, gives us his own views of preaching with power and profit to his hearers. "Whatever be said in the pulpit," he wrote, "men will not much regard, though they feel it at the time, if the minister does not say the same in private with equal earnestness in speaking with his people face to face, and it must be in our moments of most familiar intercourse with them that we are thus to put the seal to all we say in public. Familiar moments are the times when the things which are most closely twined round the heart are brought out to view, and shall we forbear, by tacit consent, to introduce the Lord that bought us into such happy hours? We must not only speak faithfully to our people in our sermons, but live faithfully for them too. Perhaps it may be found that the reason why many who preach the Gospel fully and in all earnestness are not owned of God in the conversion of souls, is to be found in their defective exhibition of grace in these easy moments of life. 'Them that honour Me, I will honour' (1 Sam. ii. 30.) It was noticed long ago that men will give you leave to preach against their sins as much as you will, if so be you will but be easy with them when you have done, and talk as they do, and live as they live. How much otherwise it was with Mr. M'Cheyne, all who knew him are witnesses."—*Memoir*, p. 76.

But I may remind the reader that besides the godly ministers of modern times who have preached in Dundee, there were several who may be here named of a former generation who were men valiant for the truth as it is in Jesus. The learned Rev. James Durham, author of *An Exposition of the Revelations* and *Discourses on the Song of Solomon*, and other works, was born in the neighbourhood of Dundee, and preached in our town about 1647. He was called "that singularly wise and faithful servant of Jesus Christ." The following account of his conversion is given in Wodrow's *Analecta* :—" He was young when he married, and was not for a while concerned about religion. He came with his lady, being by birth a gentleman, to visit his mother-in-law, who lived in the parish of Queensferry. There fell at that time a Communion to be in the Queensferry, and so the lady Duntarvie desired her son-in-law, Mr. Durham, to go and hear the sermon upon the Saturday, and for some time he would by no means go, till both his lady and his mother-in-law, with much importunity, at last prevailed with him to go. He went that day and heard very attentively. He seemed to be moved by the preacher that day, being very serious in his discourse, so that there was something wrought in Mr. Durham that day. When he came home he said to his mother-in-law, 'Mother, ye had much ado to get me to the church this day, but I will go to-morrow without your importuning me.' He went away on the Sabbath morning and heard the minister of the place preach the action sermon upon 1 Pet. ii. 7, 'Unto you, therefore, which believe He is precious, but to them which be disobedient, the stone which the builders disallowed, the same is made the head of the corner.' Mr. Durham then had these expressions about the sermon—'He commended Him, he commended Him again and again, till he made my heart and soul commend Him.' And so Mr. Durham immediately closed with Christ, and covenanted, and went down immediately to the table, and took the seal of the covenant, and after that he became a most serious man." Then he became the godly Rev. James Durham.

Afterwards, about 1716, the Rev. John Willison was an evangelical minister in Dundee, and was the author of numerous works, including *A Sacramental Directory*, and a treatise on the *Sanctification of the Sabbath*, *Letters about Revivals*; also *The Afflicted Man's Companion*, *Popery another Gospel*, *Balm of*

Gilead. Willison traces minutely, and bewails deeply, the corruptions of the Church, and expresses the most earnest longing and fervent supplication that a time of refreshing might visit Scotland ; he also concluded, from a view of prophecy, that some great revolution would take place in France about 1792, which was fearfully verified, as all Europe knows. I have read several of the works of both these good men with great pleasure and profit. I may say they are safe and sound, and calculated to be a blessing to the soul, and are likely by grace to help the believer to follow on to know the Lord from grace to glory.

And now let us mention with the deepest respect Mr. George Wishart, who preached to the people ill of the plague at the East Port, or gate of Dundee, in 1541, and was shortly thereafter burned to death by the Papists at St. Andrews, whose motto, " Semper idem " (always the same), warns us how, to this day, although they cannot now burn us in this country, yet they may seek to glide into every Protestant institution, so that by raising disputes and lawsuits, etc., they may compass their ruin.

One evening, in St. Peter's Church, Dundee, the Rev. Cæsar Malan, of Geneva, preached, pressing the people to believe, and then to live in conscious assurance of being saved, illustrating the point by the following anecdote (see *Life of Rev. W. C. Burns*, p. 116):—One day Napoleon was reviewing some troops, when the bridle of his horse slipped from his hand and the horse galloped off. A common soldier ran, and, laying hold of the bridle, brought back the horse to the Emperor's hand, who addressed the soldier, and said, "Well done, Captain!" The soldier enquired, "Of what regiment, Sire?" "Of the Guards," answered Napoleon, pleased with the instant belief in his word. The Emperor rode off. The soldier threw down his musket, and though he had no epaulettes on his shoulder, no sword by his side, nor any other mark of his advancement than the word of the Emperor, he ran and joined the staff of commanding officers. They laughed at him, and said, "What have you to do here?" He replied, "I am Captain of the Guards." They were amazed, but he said, "The Emperor has said so, and therefore I am." "In like manner," said Mr. Malan, "he that believeth on the Son hath everlasting life (John iii. 36), is not confirmed by the feelings of the believer. He ought to take the Word of God as true, because He has said it, and thus honour Him as a God of truth, and then rejoice with joy unspeakable."

I lately conversed with an aged lady, Mrs. Scott, in Newport, who remembers Mr. M'Cheyne very well. He used to come to Springhill, in the east end of Dundee, and preach in the open air, and she remembers of the crowds being round him hearing the Gospel. There were a number of conversions at that time in the district, both amongst the young and the old. Mr. M'Cheyne joined with a prayer meeting in the neighbourhood, which was attended by this lady's mother and herself, for young folks went to it as well as the grown-up people. One lady who attended lost two of her daughters while bathing, and was much overcome under the preaching of Mr. M'Cheyne, as it came to her with power. "My

mother was a godly woman," said my friend, "and
sat over the Bible a great deal. In the evening she
wished to be alone over her Bible, and she left us for
her own retirement. Then at the prayer-meeting
it was psalms and paraphases which were sung.
Hymns were not much in use in these young days,
except in the Methodist Church, where we went on
the Sabbath mornings to the Sabbath-school. Mr.
M'Cheyne was a delicate-looking lad, and had a very
loving manner. His memory is fragrant to this day,
and her friend, mentioned above, said she had never
heard any one like Mr. M'Cheyne. In these days
the Fast Thursday was kept like a Sabbath by my
mother ; now it is kept very differently ; and even
the Preparation Saturday and the Thanksgiving
Monday were very well kept, the shops mostly shut
during the services, and everything very quiet."

So, you see, the boys and girls in the east end got
a blessing, and the boys and girls in the west end got
a blessing. We did not know theology ; we just
loved Jesus. As it is written, " I love them that love
Me, and those that seek Me early shall find Me "
(Prov. viii. 17).

> " We heard of a Saviour whose love was so great
>   That He laid down His life on the tree ;
> The thorns they were placed on His beautiful brow
>   To save a poor sinner like me.

> " This love, so amazing, it broke my hard heart,
>   And brought me, dear Jesus, to Thee.
> And I knew when I came Thou didst not cast me out,
>   But pardoned a sinner like me."

He *died* for us, so we have loved Him ; we have

sought Him, and we have found Him! And though memory is not without its blurs and dark spots, we could almost say with Lavater: "Oh! that we could weep ourselves back to the simplicity of early days."

The rose has its thorn, the morning has its cloud, the evening has its weariness, but "He knoweth our frame, He remembereth that we are dust" (Ps. ciii. 14), so we now just apply to our never-failing Friend, the Lord Jesus Christ, that His own precious blood may wash all these stains away. Amen.

XVII

"VERY happy in my work," Mr. M'Cheyne wrote in his diary, Sabbath, 30th September 1838. "Too little prayer in the morning. Must try to get early to bed on Saturday, that I may rise a great while before day."

These early hours of prayer on Sabbath he endeavoured to have all his life; not for study, but for prayer. He never laboured at his sermons on Sabbath. That day he kept for its original end, the refreshment of his soul.

Old Mr. John Mathewson, one of Mr. M'Cheyne's elders, used to have prayer in the early mornings, and he would sometimes give me a familiar touch and say, "There's no a day but I mind you." I like early prayer myself, and hundreds of times I have had it. The day I pen these lines I had a blessed time of prayer before the dawning of the day.

When Mr. M'Cheyne was away to Palestine, he preached twenty-seven times in twenty-four different places. On arriving home he was warmly welcomed by his people. "I wish you had been with me last night," he wrote to a friend. "When I was away, the people agreed to meet twice a week in the lower school-room to pray for me, and now that I have come back we have continued the meetings. The school is quite crammed. Such sweet, loud singing of praise I never heard, and many tears. I stood by a poor Socialist in the agonies of death to-day. He was quite well yesterday. He anxiously wished me to come and pray. Oh! to be ready when the Bridegroom comes. Farewell. Peace from above fill your soul. When a traveller passes very rapidly through a country, the eye has no time to rest upon the different objects in it, so that when he comes to the end of his journey no distinct impressions have been made upon his mind; he has only a confused notion of the country through which he has travelled. This explains how it is that death, judgment, eternity makes so little impression upon most men's minds. Most people never stop to think, but hurry on through life, and find themselves in eternity before they have once put the question, 'What must I do to be saved?' More souls are lost through want of consideration than in any other way. The reason why men are not awakened and made anxious for their souls is that the devil never gives them time to consider. Therefore God cries, 'Stop, poor sinner, stop and think. Consider your ways. Oh, that you were wise, that you understood this, that you considered your latter end.' And again He cries, 'Israel doth not know, My people doth not consider.' (Considers: to revolve in my mind.) In the same way does the devil try to make the children of God doubt if there be a Providence. He hurries them away to the shop and market. 'Lose no time,' he says, 'but make money.' Therefore God cries, 'Stop, poor sinner, stop and think.' And Jesus says, 'Consider the lilies of the field, how they grow; consider the ravens, which have neither storehouse nor barn.' In the same way does the devil try to make the children of God live uncomfortable and unholy lives. He beguiles them away from simply looking to Jesus; he hurries them away to look at a thousand other things, as he led Peter walking on the sea to look round at the waves. But God says; 'Consider the Apostle and High Priest of your profession; look unto Me and be ye saved; run your race, looking unto Jesus; consider Christ, the same yesterday, and to-day, and for ever.' 'He is above yon clouds and above yon sky.' Oh, that you would stand gazing up into heaven, not with bodily eye, but with the eye of faith! Oh, what a wonderful thing is the eye of faith! It sees beyond the stars, it pierces to the throne of God, and there it looks on the face of Jesus making intercession for us, whom, having not seen, we love. Some people think there is no joy in religion; it is a gloomy thing. 'When a young person becomes a Christian,' they would say, 'alas! he must bid farewell to pleasure, farewell to the joys of youth, farewell to a merry heart. He must exchange these pleasures for reading of the Bible and dry sermon books, for a life of gravity and preciseness.' This is what the world says. What does the Bible say? 'I sat down under His shadow with great delight.' Some people are afraid of anything like joy in religion. They have none themselves, and they do not love to see it in others. Their religion is something like the stars, very high and very clear, but very cold. When they see tears of anxiety, or tears of joy, they cry out,

'Enthusiasm—enthusiasm!' Well, then, to the law
and to the testimony. 'I sat down under His
shadow with great delight.' Is this enthusiasm? Oh,
Lord, evermore give us this enthusiasm! 'May the
God of Hope fill you with all joy and peace in
believing.' If it be really in sitting under the shadow
of Christ, let there be no bounds to your joy. Oh!
if God would but open your eyes and give you
simple childlike faith to look to Jesus, to sit under
His shadow, then would songs of joy rise from all
our dwellings. 'Rejoice in the Lord alway: and
again I say, Rejoice.' Often when I look at a large
town like Dundee, and see so few converted to Christ,
my heart sickens within me. Although there has
been so much blessing, yet such masses of ungodly
families! But oh! cheer up; Christ shall have His
full share. Learn the power of His blood. It blots
out the sins of that multitude (Rev. vii. 9), sins of
every name and dye. Why not yours? Oh! when
such a glorious company are saved, why should you
be lost? Some believers are much surprised when
they are called to suffer. They thought they would
do some great thing for God, but all that God
permits them to do is to suffer. Go round every one
in glory, every one has a different story. One was
persecuted in his family. Another was visited by
sore pains and humbling disease, neglected by the
world. Another was bereaved of children, another
had all these afflictions meeting in one. Mark, all
are brought out of them. It was a dark cloud, but
it passed away; the water was deep, but they have
reached the other side. Some good men cry, 'Flee,

flee,' without showing the sinner what he is to flee from; and again they cry, 'Come, come,' without showing plainly the way of pardon and peace. These men act as men would do who should run through the streets, crying 'Fire, fire,' without telling where. If a neighbour's house were on fire, would we not cry aloud and use every exertion? If a friend were drowning, would we be ashamed to strain every nerve to save him? But, alas! the souls of our neighbours are even now on their way to everlasting burnings, they are ready to be devoured in the depths of perdition. Oh! shall we be less earnest to save their bodies? 'When Jesus came near and beheld the city, He wept over it.' How earnest was Paul: 'I ceased not to warn every one, night and day, with tears.' Such was George Whitfield; that great man scarcely ever preached without being melted into tears. Ah! how we shall be amazed at our coldness when we get to heaven."—*Memoir and Remains.*

The late Mr. Fuller of Kettering was wont to tell the following anecdote, which he had from the lips of the person. A young man, a native of Norwich, was walking one morning with a party of other young men. They met an old woman who pretended to tell fortunes, and that they might fully qualify her to tell their fortunes, they first made her intoxicated with spirituous liquor. This young man was told he would live to an old age, and see his children and children's children, etc. etc. The young man then went off to hear Mr. Whitfield.

In the course of the sermon on Matt. iii. 7, "O, generation of vipers, who hath warned you to flee from the wrath to come," Mr. Whitfield abruptly broke off, paused for a few moments, then burst into a flood of tears, lifted up his his hands and eyes, and exclaimed, 'Oh, my hearers, the wrath to come, the wrath to come, the wrath to come!'" "These words," said the young man, "sank into my heart like lead in the waters. I wept, and when the sermon was ended retired alone. For days and weeks I could think of little else. These awful words followed me wherever I went: 'The wrath to come!—the wrath to come!'" The issue was that the young man soon after made a public profession of religion, and in a little time became a preacher. He himself related the foregoing circumstances to Mr. Fuller.—*Life of Selina, Countess of Huntingdon.*

"'If,' said the dying Payson,' Mr. M‘Cheyne continues, 'if ministers only saw the preciousness of Christ, they would not be able to refrain from clapping their hands with joy and exclaiming, "I am a minister of Christ."' 'And the want of ministerial success,' says Robinson, 'is a tremendous circumstance never to be contemplated without horror. Satan aims his fiery darts at ministers. If he can only make you a covetous minister, or a lover of pleasure, or a lover of good eating, then he has ruined your ministry for ever.'"

Mr. M‘Cheyne has left several very nice hymns to us in his beautiful little book, *Songs of Zion.* Some are for the young, and I dare say the one beginning, "Like mist on the mountain," may be considered as one of his best, which he wrote 1st January 1837. I would say, in his love for Jesus, or when tried by affliction, nearly every Christian becomes a poet. And on coming to the valley of the shadow of death, very gracious, poetic feeling may spring up in his heart. The dying bed in life's last hours had often been the " Poets' Corner " to the believers; the Divine ante-chamber of heaven, where his glorious Lord meets him to take him to his home beyond the skies.

But Mr. M'Cheyne did not forget the ethics of his position, the doctrine of morality, and delivering of precepts of morality.

It has not always to be moral essays, but morality has always to be hand in hand with spirituality in a minister; and the reason a pastor sometimes may fail to be successful with His people is that they may say, " He is very good in the pulpit, but look at his life ! " May the Lord help us all to set a wise and good and holy example to those around us, and not outrage any one by our thoughtless, imprudent lives, for it is written, " My servant shall deal prudently " (Isa. lii. 13). Also, " Let not your good be evil spoken of."

February 5, Sabbath, he writes:—" After hearing Mr. Martin of St. George's, Edinburgh—Oh! how humble, yet how diligent; how lowly, yet how watchful; how prayerful, night and day it becomes me to be when I see such men. Help, Father, Son, and Spirit.

" Again saw the dying woman.

" Oh, when will I plead with my tears and inward yearnings over sinners? Oh, compassionate Lord, give me Thy gentle Spirit, that neither strives nor cries."

Again he writes:—"Be not deceived, my young friends, the world has many sensual and many sinful delights—the delights of eating and drinking and wearing gay clothes, the delights of revelry and the dance. God requires His redeemed ones to be holy. If you are His brethren, He will have you righteous, holy men. He requires you to do justly, to be just in your dealings between man and man. This is one of His own glorious pictures. He is a just God. Shall not the Judge of all the earth do right? He is my Rock, and there is no unrighteousness in Him. Are you come to Him by Jesus? He requires you to reflect His image. Are you His child? You must be like Him. Oh, brethren, be exact in your dealings. Be like your God. Take care of dishonesty; take care of trickery in your business. Take care of crying up your goods when selling them, and crying them down when buying them. 'It is naught, it is naught with the buyer, but when he is gone his way, then he boasteth.' It shall not be so among you. God requires you to do justly. Look as much to Him for sanctification as for justification."

> "So will your walk be close with God,
>   Calm and serene your frame;
> So purer light shall mark the road
>   That leads you to the Lamb."

Mr. M'Cheyne was requested by the Presbytery of Aberdeen to give some account of the revival in Dundee, and he wrote as follows:—"The previous character of those who seem to have been converted was very various. I could name not a few in the highest ranks of life that seem evidently to have become new creatures, who previously lived a worldly life, though unmarked by open wickedness. Many, again, who were before nominal Christians, are now living ones. I could name, however, far more who have been turned from the paths of open sin and profligacy, and have found pardon and purity in the blood of the Lamb, and by the Spirit of our God, so that we can say of them, as Paul said to the Corinthians, 'Such were some of you, but ye are washed, but ye are sanctified, but ye are purified,' etc. I often think, when conversing with some of these, that the change they have undergone might be enough to convince an atheist that there is a God, or an infidel that there is a Saviour. During the autumn of 1839, no fewer than from six hundred to seven hundred came to converse with the ministers about their souls. Indeed, eternity alone can reveal the true number of the Lord's hidden ones amongst us."—*Memoir*, pp. 545, 546.

I like Mr. M'Cheyne for his attention and love for the young. When he came home from the Holy Land, there were several young people's prayer-meetings, and he requested some particulars about them, as I mentioned in a former chapter. A young boy named Tom Brown and I were deputed, or it was arranged somehow for us to call with the paper to give to Mr. M'Cheyne, as I have already told in a former sketch, but will repeat it in case some reader did not notice it. We called at his house, and were taken into the kitchen by the servant, who went across the lobby, knocked at a door, when Mr.

M'Cheyne came to where we two boys were standing; but I cannot remember any more, perhaps the excitement drove the memory out of my mind. I know young people were much cared for by him, and have been told by some who are now old and grey-headed how kind and good he was to them, and helped them to the Saviour.

"How many," he wrote, "have had a time of awakening in childhood—when they were prayed over by a believing mother, or warned by a believing father, or taught by a faithful Sabbath-school teacher. How many have had deep impressions made at the Sabbath-school; but they have passed away like the morning cloud and early dew. At their first communion, when they first spoke to a minister about their soul, and heard his piercing questions and faithful warnings, when they got their token from his hand, when they first received the bread and wine and sat at the table of the Lord, they trembled, the tear dimmed their eye, they went home to pray. But soon it wore away. The world, pleasure, cares, involved the mind, and all was gone but the cloud and the dew. Not all at once, but by degrees he gives up secret prayer. At one time he has been out in company, another time kept long at business, another time he is sleeping, and so by degrees he gives it up altogether. He is lively in his attendance on the Word; but when his concern wears away he begins to weary of the week-day service, then of the Sabbath. Then, perhaps, he seeks a more careless ministry, where he may slumber on till death and judgment. Ah! this has been the course of thousands in this place. God mourns over their case. 'O Ephraim, what shall I do unto thee? O Judah, what shall I do unto thee? for your goodness is as a morning cloud, and as the early dew it goeth away' (Hos. vi. 4)."

So you see, in these beautiful and earnest words of Mr. M'Cheyne, how he longed for the salvation of souls, and used the means for their conversion. Oh, how we need more men like him nowadays to preach the Truth and lead us to Jesus! Evermore give us faithful and true ministers, O Lord, to advance Thy cause and glorify Thy name. We need more of such men as uphold the truth of the Bible in these days of unbelief, trial, and darkness. And we need more of them who will guide the young to the Saviour, and teach them to grow up to honour and the fear of the Lord. For the time is short—eternity is at hand: prepare to meet thy God.

The Rev. John Scott of Auchterless has also a nice word for revival: "I remember preaching in St. Peter's twenty-three years ago," he wrote, " and feeling a certain awe as I entered the pulpit which this man of God had occupied.

"What a need there is at the present time for a revival such as took place in his day. It is time to enquire what hinders it. There is a great lack of earnest intercessory prayer, 'Behold, the Lord's hand is not shortened that it cannot save,' etc. (Isa. lix. 1)."

And the Rev. John Dewar, of Kilmartin, Argyle-shire, writes me a few interesting lines of his visit to Jacob's Well in the Holy Land. It was this well

into which the Rev. Dr. Andrew Bonar's Bible fell,
and Mr. M'Cheyne wrote a few verses on the
subject :—

> " My own loved Bible, must I part from thee,
>   Companion of my toils by land and sea ;
>   Man of my counsels, soother of distress,
>   Guide of my steps through this world's wilderness?
>   In darkest nights, a lantern to my feet ;
>   In gladsome days, as dropping honey sweet.
>   When first I parted from my quiet home,
>   At thy command, for Israel's good to roam,
>   Thy gentle voice said, 'For Jerusalem pray,
>   So shall Jehovah prosper all thy way.'
>   When through the lonely wilderness we strayed,
>   Sighing in vain for palm-trees' cooling shade,
>   Thy words of comfort hushed each rising fear,
>   'The shadow of thy mighty Rock is near.'
>   And when we pitched our tent on Judah's hills,
>   Or thoughtful mused beside Siloa's rills ;
>   Whene'er we climbed Mount Olivet, to gaze
>   Upon the sea, where stood in ancient days
>   The heaven-struck Sodom . . .
>   Sweet record of the past, to faith's glad eyes,
>   Sweet promiser of glories yet to rise ! " [1]

" We left Jerusalem," Mr. Dewar writes, " on
Monday morning, about 6.30, 22nd February 1908,
and travelled to Nablous, arriving there about 6 p.m.

" It was a lovely day, rather chilly in the morning,
but very warm later. We missed a view of Mount
Hermon, as it was too foggy.

" The present road does not pass close to some of
the interesting spots; but we were shown Bethel,

---

[1] It is a somewhat curious occurrence, that the remnants of this Bible
were found, and drawn up from the bottom of the well, in July 1843, by
Dr. Wilson and his fellow-traveller, who employed a Samaritan from
Sychar to descend and examine the well.

Nob, Shiloh, etc., and halted about mid-day at the boundary line between Judæa and Samaria, and passed the tombs of Eleazar and Phinehas. There was rather a scene on the way. As we were nearing Jacob's Well, some of our men, to avoid the rough roads which had just been covered with fresh metal, trespassed on the corn-fields, which the natives resisted and came up with fire-arms; but they were soon put into good humour by the usual backsheesh, which seemed to have been the sole object of their threatening demonstration. We visited Jacob's Well. After having performed the journey from Jerusalem, we could well imagine how fatigued our Lord would be on his arrival at the well. How many have since gazed down at the well, as Dr. Bonar and M'Cheyne did, when the former dropped his Bible into the well. Some of the visitors carried away with them some of the water in small phials; but my own feelings were more in the direction of the *living water* which the whole scene suggested.

> " 'Thou art the well that springeth
> From cisterns out of sight;
> With music sweet it singeth,
> Uprising day and night.

> " 'Oh! may that living Fountain
> Make melody in me,
> Till in God's holy mountain
> Its sacred source I see.'

" How deeply M'Cheyne drew from the Living Fountain, you yourself have indicated in the sketches you have published about him."—JOHN DEWAR, *5th January* 1910.

I already mentioned that Mr. M'Cheyne was very pleased when the Rev. George Lewis was appointed to St. David's Church, Dundee. Mr. Lewis gave the use of his church, which was perhaps the largest in Dundee, that a week or so of revival meetings might be held, and was very friendly with Mr. M'Cheyne. Mr. Lewis was my own dear pastor, then a man of great power and sound judgment. A lover of the young, and much esteemed by his people, whom he often visited, he gave lectures in the town on religious and social questions, and was earnest as an educational reformer, a lover of the Lord's day, and was much concerned about the evils of the drink traffic in the town. Much regret was expressed by his flock when he accepted a call to Ormiston near Edinburgh, and some of his old people revere his memory to this day.

XVIII

THERE is sweet and lovely memory about the name of Robert Murray M'Cheyne, which illustrates the scripture in Prov. x. 7, "The memory of the just is blessed." And Dr. Andrew Bonar, his biographer, used to say, "There is a fragrance about M'Cheyne's grave." And, besides having visited it myself, I have often, in passing along the street, cast my eyes towards it, I daresay generally with a deep impression of the sacredness of the spot where the dust of the dear minister lies. One evening, when Mr. D. L. Moody was preaching in St. Peter's, Dundee, he passed out by the grave, which is at the west end of the church. A young Dundee lady, Miss S., was standing beside it. "Have you found Christ yet?" he asked her. "No," she replied. "Well, come to my room to-morrow and I will speak with you," said he. "No, I must have Him to-night," was her reply. Mr. Moody then opened up the way of salvation to her wondering gaze, and her heart responded. She received Christ as her Saviour and her God, and left the grave rejoicing. Mr. Moody had to hurry down to St. Mark's Church to address a second meeting, where, I understand, he related this beautiful story, so touching and so true.

A Christian friend, Mr. A. H. Stephen, Dundee, wrote to me about some young people's meetings in Dundee, and refers to Mr. M'Cheyne in the following terms:—"Thanks for your sketch of Robert Murray M'Cheyne, which I read with interest. When I was in America in 1903, I called on Mr. John Wanna-maker, of Philadelphia, and he told me that there was one man whom he admired more than George Washington, and that was M'Cheyne." Certainly a remarkable testimony from an American.

Mr. Duncan, another old Dundee friend, wrote to me:—"My recollection of M'Cheyne is very hazy. I mind of being on a visit to Dundee, and a friend taking me to St. Peter's. It was crowded, and many weeping; and I wondered very much at what I saw and heard, being so different from the country church at Cupar."

After M'Cheyne's return from visiting Palestine, on a mission of enquiry on behalf of the Jews, he preached a sermon from Rom. i. 16, "To the Jew first." "In many respects," he said, "Scotland may be called God's second Israel. No other land has its Sabbath as Scotland has; no other land has the Bible as Scotland has; no other land has the Gospel preached free as the air we breathe, fresh as the stream from the everlasting hills. Oh, then, think for a moment, you who sit under the shade of faithful ministers and yet remain unconcerned and unconverted, and are not brought to sit under the shade of Christ—think how like your wrath will be to that of the unbelieving Jew! And think again of the marvellous grace of Christ, that the Gospel is first to you. Should we not grave Israel upon the palms of our hands, and resolve that through our mercy they also may obtain mercy?"

He mentioned that in almost all the countries which they visited, it was remarkable that while you dare not do anything for the souls of the general public, the only door left open to the Christian missionary was the door of preaching to the Jews. "No man cares for their souls, and therefore you may carry the Gospel to them freely" (*Memoir*, p. 494). After reading Mr. M'Cheyne's *Life*, or his *Narrative of a Mission to the Jews*, most people would likely be deeply interested in their welfare, especially the salvation of their souls. Perhaps the first Jew whom I ever met said to me, as we walked the deck of a steamer, "I consider the man whom you call Jesus Christ was an impostor." I was greatly shocked, as you may well suppose. Surely it becomes us who are believers, and who are saved through the blood of the Lamb, earnestly to labour for their conversion! For, upon the heart of the dear Jew the dark veil of unbelief is still present, as when they cried out on that awful day, "His blood be on us and on our children. Away with Him! Crucify Him! Crucify Him!"

> "Fair as a beauteous tender flower
>   Amidst the desert grows;
> So, slighted by a rebel race,
>   The heavenly Saviour rose.
> Rejected and despised of men,
>   Behold a man of woe!
> Grief was His close companion still,
>   Through all His life below.

"Wronged and oppressed, how meekly He
  In patient silence stood,
Mute as the peaceful, harmless lamb,
  When brought to shed its blood.
He died to bear the guilt of men,
  That sin might be forgiven :
He lives to bless them and defend,
  And plead their cause in heaven."

Paraphrase xxv.

My esteemed friend, Mr. James E. Mathieson of London, who is a great worker amongst the Jews, and President of the Prayer Union for Israel, wrote me lately as follows:—"Thanks for your note and the accompanying print about the revival work in Dundee in the days of Murray M'Cheyne and Andrew Bonar. The last-named, as well as his brother Horatius, I knew very well, and have had under my roof. One remarkable thing you do not refer to, namely, the preaching of William C. Burns during the absence of M'Cheyne in the Holy Land. For some time M'Cheyne had been preaching in St. Peter's without indication of much blessing—'sowing in tears'—but William Burns, taking the place of the absent pastor, began to witness showers of blessing, in which many people pressed into the kingdom. A poor woman, Jessie Veitch, was saved at that time, and became later a Bible - woman in Edinburgh, through the kind intervention of the Barbour family. After M'Cheyne's return home, William Burns offered himsef in 1847 to our English Presbyterian Church as our first missionary to China, and exercised a deep influence over J. Hudson Taylor prior to the founding of the China Inland Mission. Burns went about evangelising, wearing the Chinese dress, found his way from South China, where first he saw a little fruit of his labours; further and further northwards, laying down his life at Mukden, in Manchuria, and there was buried. The influence of his devoted career has been felt in China amongst two generations of succeeding missionaries, including thirty ladies of our Women's Missionary Association, of which my wife is President. There is now a large native church in South China and in Formosa. When M'Cheyne's *Memoir* was published, it was much read by Church of England evangelicals. How changed is the Scotland of to-day from what it was in the earlier period I have referred to! In some respects we may say 'Ichabod!' (the glory has departed), but God is able to revive us again. Oh, that it might be soon!—Believe me, yours sincerely in Christ Jesus, (Signed) J. E. MATHIESON."

In conclusion about the Jews here, I now insert two verses of the 123rd Psalm :—

> " Now Israel
>   May say, and that truly,
>   If that the Lord
>   Had not our cause maintain'd ;
>   If that the Lord
>   Had not our right sustain'd,
>   When cruel men
>   Against us furiously,
>   Rose up in wrath
>   To make of us their prey :
>
> " Then certainly
>   They had devour'd us all,
>   And swallow'd quick,
>   For ought that we could deem :

"Such was their rage,
    As we might well esteem.
And as fierce floods
    Before them all things drown,
So had they brought
    Our soul to death quite down."

I have received a nice letter from Miss Mudie of Montrose, as to her mother's memories of Mr. M'Cheyne.

"Almost the only thing," she writes, "my mother could tell was at being present at a Communion service in St. Peter's, when visiting her brother, Mr. Caird, who was an elder in his congregation, and the wonderfully solemn impression made on her mind: how it seemed the very gate of heaven to believers; and then how, at the close, Mr. M'Cheyne pleaded with unsaved souls, with all the earnestness of one who realised their danger, to come to the Saviour ere it was too late. We have also, again and again, heard her speak of a pastoral visit he made to my uncle's (Mr. Caird's) home, and how the very way he read the Scripture so impressed it on her heart that never was that portion read but she remembered his reading of it on that occasion. The portion of Scripture was 2 Cor. i. 10: 'Who delivered us from so great a death, and doth deliver; in whom we trust that He will yet deliver us.' I think that was the only time she had the privilege of being with him."

The Rev. Wm. Young, of Newport-on-Tay, wrote me lately as follows:—"Many thanks for your kindness in sending me *The Scottish Reformer* to Callander. I have read with great interest your article on revivals in Dundee in the days of

M'Cheyne. What God has done in the past He can do in the present, and will do it if we only open our hearts to His Spirit."

The Rev. Alexander Goodfellow, of South Ronaldshay, Orkney, wrote me lately:—"I return the enclosed article as you desire, after I have enjoyed the perusal of it; a most precious article concerning that saint of saints, M'Cheyne. The letter," he continues, "from Mrs. Nairn is a most valuable one, and might be added afterwards as an appendix to his life. It is good to gather up these fragments; nothing concerning him might be lost, for all his words were so savoury."

I am very glad to be able to add here a few more incidents from my dear friend Mrs. Nairn, now on her death-bed, which friends will read with pleasure and profit while she still suffers, according to the will of God, as it is written, "For unto you it is given in the behalf of Christ not only to believe on Him, but also to suffer for His sake" (Phil. i. 29.) "Still suffer a great deal, and have very weary and restless nights. I often think of the dying man that Dr. Wilson went to see. He asked him if he went often to Jesus. 'Na, na,' he replied, 'I'm no able; but He comes to me.' He is the Friend that never leaves us, and is always near. On looking back to M'Cheyne's days, he one day asked me to go to a lady's house and inquire if she expected another minister to be present at her mother's funeral, as he had the prayer-meeting at St. David's that day. I had to meet him there with the answer that she expected *him* to have the service in the house; then we went together, when

his remarks were so full of love and sympathy, just
like his Master's.   We then visited an only daughter
on her death-bed.   His greeting to her was, 'Well,
Mary, how are you to-day?'   She replied, 'My head
is sore, sore.'   He put his hand so tenderly on her
head, and requested for something to shield her from
the fire.   I have never forgotten the first words of his
prayer then, namely, 'Dear Father, put Thou Thy
left hand under her sore, sore head, and may Thy
right hand support and strengthen her.'   One of the
last sermons I heard him preach, he said: 'Soon
another minister will stand in this pulpit, and others
will sit in these pews; oh! where will your souls be?
These walls will witness that I have put before you
life and death, heaven and hell.   Oh! why not decide
for the Lord now?   He is waiting to receive you.'   I
am delighted," writes Mrs. Nairn to me, "to read so
many testimonies to the Bible in the *Soul Winner*.
His word and promise I have found never fail.   Every
trial we have to pass through is sent by our blessed
Redeemer and Refiner, who sits at the furnace door
and gives in more than I need, to draw me closer to
Himself.   To think we shall be like Him, when we
see Him as He is!   May the Lord bless and use you
more and more in His work."

May the Lord bless our dear aged friend also, as
she is now passing through Jordan's stream.   As it
is written, "When thou passest through the waters, I
will be with thee, and through the rivers, they shall
not overflow thee" (Isa. xliii. 2).   My dear friend
Mrs Nairn has now left us for the glory land on high.

Dr. Stewart, of Murtle, Aberdeen, is interested also

in the old times about which I am writing, as I had
the following from him at one time:—" I now thank
you for your second article.   It is exceedingly interesting, and especially so because of your own personal
experience in the things related.   All who have recollections about the times and work of M'Cheyne
must take great interest in such articles."   The dear
doctor has also passed away.

My good old friend, Mrs. Smith of Methven, who
was a close follower of the dear minister of St. Peter's,
Dundee, again writes me as follows:—" I am always
glad to see anything about my dear old minister, Mr.
M'Cheyne.   I love to hear his name, and was pleased
to spend the little time with you that afternoon to
talk over the blessed things he had done in his short
days upon earth.   One thing he always did, in reading
the Word, or preaching the Word, he explained the
doctrine thereof, which has been a great blessing to
me and has kept me steadfast in the faith, even in
the midst of much error on every side, these many
years.   Nothing has moved my soul from the Word
of the living God and the glorious Gospel of Jesus
Christ.   I must tell you," she continues, "what I
heard him say once in a sermon.   He said he
believed that a man would ride on horseback a
whole day in our lovely Scotland and would not
hear one Gospel sermon.   Another good way he had,
of dividing the sermon into heads—first, second, and
third, and everybody got their portion.   A bit to the
saved, a bit to the unsaved, a bit to the anxious soul,
so that no one need be deceived.   Thanks be unto
God for our teachers," she adds, "and for all the

books and other helps we have had by the way to cheer and comfort us in our journey homeward. With best wishes that every blessing may be to you and yours, till we all meet together in the morning.—With love from   (Signed)   J. SMITH."

Thus you see how Mr. M'Cheyne's life of prayer and holiness gave him the power, so that his words are taking effect in the hearts and lives of his hearers to this day.

"The power of personal holiness in your minister," wrote Rev. Duncan M'Gregor in his *Shepherd of Israel*, "is a great confirmation to the truth spoken from the pulpit; but when sallies against the Bible, or improprieties generally appear, all influence for good seems gone" (P. 250).

And I think a minister ought to have influence with the young, with young men and maidens—oh, how important! Lead them in the way of temperance and godliness. And take a deep, fatherly care over the very young; they do not seem to have the same chances nowadays. Fathers, as a rule, are *never seen walking with their children now*, instructing them and guiding them in their young days. So children are apt in such cases to grow up in sports and play without the sense of authority and respect for superiors, and thus the sense of parental control gets obliterated, and the Divine command and injunction, "Children, obey your parents," may get to be unknown. I would humbly say, as one who has, by grace, kept these important matters in view and in constant practice, that I am now amply rewarded by respect, obedience, and love, and so, most earnestly

do I, in a humble way, call the attention of parents
and ministers to the above very important matters.

> Give not strangers all your smiles,
>   Bring a handful of them home!
> Satan watches with his wiles,
>   To destroy, when parents roam.

And be cautious with your dear children, and not
lead them astray!   Mr. M'Cheyne was very particular
against those who were "lovers of pleasure more than
lovers of God."   "The theatre," he said on a Communion Sabbath, "is one of its temples; there it sits
enthroned.   The tavern is another, where its reeling,
staggering votaries sing its praise.   What have you
to do with these?   How dare you cross the threshold
of a theatre or a tavern any more?   What! the Spirit
of God amid the wanton songs of a theatre, or the
boisterous merriment of a tavern?   Shame on such
practical blasphemy!   No; leave them, dear friends,
to be cages of devils, and of every unclean and hateful
bird.   You must never cross their threshold any more.
What shall I say of games?—cards, dice, dancing.   I
will only say this, that if you love them, you have
never tasted the joys of the new creature.   What
shall I say of dress?   The joy of being in Christ is
so sweet that it makes all other joys insipid, dull,
listless."—*Memoir and Remains*.

And there is plenty of scope for ministers acting
as temperance guides to the young, by Bands of
Hope and juvenile societies, with a view to give
them an inextinguishable horror of drink and the
drink traffic, which, alas! meets our gaze at every
step, as it were, in our dear native land.   And it is

bad abroad also, as I have observed in some of the northern countries of Europe. And when we were in Newark, New Jersey, U.S.A., our kind host, Mr. Stanford, informed us that in a radius of one hundred yards there are twenty saloons, and in the German district forty in a radius of one hundred yards.

Reader and friend! be warned, be entreated to flee from the temptations of drink and evil company, whether male or female. Fly from temptations of the devil as for your life. "For it is the solemn duty of every Christian," says an able writer, "to warn the perishing millions around him" (*Travels*, p. 110). Let us listen to the voice of heavenly wisdom in God's Word, and He will bless us :—

> " She guides the young with innocence
>   In pleasure's paths to tread ;
> A crown of glory she bestows
>   Upon the hoary head.
>
> " According as her labours rise,
>   So her rewards increase ;
> Her ways are ways of pleasantness,
>   And all her paths are peace."

Paraphrase xi.

And what is to be done for dear neglected children, boys and girls of godless, careless, drunken parents? It is really somewhat heartrending to see crowds of them on the streets of our large towns just running wild, and father or mother, perhaps, glad to get them sent off to training ships or reformatories or such like, so as to be out of their way. May the Lord help the children and direct us what is to be done for them.

The very day I wrote some of the above lines I had been in Mr. M'Cheyne's study, where he had likely composed those solemn words of warning. And I had also prayed in the very chamber where he died, and where he yielded up his immortal spirit to Him who gave it. How solemn to be there! How affecting to visit the room where he, at the first of this closing scene of his life, requested to be left alone for half an hour. When his servant entered the room again, Mr. M'Cheyne exclaimed with a joyful voice, " My soul is escaped as a bird out of the snare of the fowler ; the snare is broken, and I am escaped." His countenance as he said this bespoke inward peace, and afterwards, when taking a little refreshment, he gave thanks " for strength in the time of weakness ; for light in the time of darkness ; for joy in the time of sorrow ; for comforting us in all our tribulations, that we may be able to comfort those that are in any trouble by the comfort wherewith we ourselves are comforted of God."

And while these solemn scenes were being witnessed long ago in M'Cheyne's dying chamber, we are reminded how his dear assistant, William C. Burns, was labouring on, and was by and by to sail as a missionary for China, and be greatly used of God in that distant heathen land.

One day he boarded a British ship with his Chinese dress on, when the captain came to him, and said, " Well, Mr. Chinaman, what do you want ? " Mr. Burns replied with his plain Scotch tongue, and they were very soon in the cabin talking together over home affairs.   Then when he in after years was dying, he was saying, "God will carry on the work. Ah no, I have no fears of that."   And, praise God! He has been carrying it on in the glorious Manchuria revival.   It is just about a week since I had prayer with Dr. Christie of Manchuria, and he told me it was going on still.

XIX

WHEN the Holy Spirit is poured out on a church or district, the people love to meet together, to have times of devotion, reading of Scripture, and praising the Lord in psalms and hymns and spiritual songs. As far back as the Psalmist's day, we have a description of this (Ps. cx. 3) :—

> "A willing people in Thy day
> Of pow'r shall come to Thee,
> In holy beauties from morn's womb ;
> Thy youth like dew shall be."

"Like new-born babes, innocent, pure, in holy simplicity, sanctified by the influence of the Spirit" (Weiss, p. 390).

"More than the dew from the womb of the morning is the dew of Thy progeny—that is, Thy children, begotten to Thee, through the Gospel" (Bishop Louth).

And then we have the nice explanation of the passage by my favourite commentator, John Trapp, 1647 :—"The influence of God's Spirit and His presence in holy ordinances is of that generating and enlivening virtue that the dew of the teeming morning is to the seeds and plants of the earth."

So the Spirit being poured out on Mr. M'Cheyne's church and people in 1839, they would meet together and pray and call on the name of the Lord with very great delight and joy. They were revived and quickened, and straightway proceeded to use that holy violence which a Christian is to put forth in the pursuit after glory, as an old writer quaintly says on the subject. And at that time the ministers also of Dundee had the Divine influences and gracious power of the Spirit poured out upon them as well as upon their people, and a weekly prayer-meeting was commenced for themselves, and carried on with great spirit, to seek more and more that the presence and power of God would be their portion and the portion of their people. I am reminded of this by lately receiving a nice letter from the Rev. John Riddell of Glasgow, telling me that a number of ministers there meet each Monday "to cry to God for a spirit-wrought revival, personal, family, congregational, world-wide." In returning my sketch, No. 16, he says: "It is full of interest to me; especially interesting are your reminiscences of the meetings for the young. The blessed Spirit always works on the same glorious plan, and when there is an awakening the dear young people always come in for a large share of the blessing. I do not remember that I have heard of these before."

A number of us boys in these old times frequently had prayer-meetings in a quiet place in my father's factory. It happened this way. A lot of us boys and girls were going home from the Sabbath-school, but we did not go to St. Peter's Church, where Mr. M'Cheyne preached; we went to St. David's. Some one said we should have a prayer-meeting, as I

recollect, and we asked my parents if we could have
a room to meet in. I well recollect it, as it was
named the mid-room. Some verses of the Bible
having been read, I think by me, one of the girls said
she would pray, and so the work began. At that
time there were many meetings held among old and
young, and in the Sabbath morning meetings, prayer
would be made for blessing on the work of the day.
I remember that in our meetings we used to pray
that we would be kept faithful; quoting the verse,
Luke ix. 62, of not "putting our hand to the plough
and looking back," i.e. being backsliders. I asked a
ploughman lately, as he was ploughing in a field,
what would happen if he looked back. He said he
would make a crook, or crooked bit, in the furrow.
So, reader, we have not to look back, and make
crooked places in the furrows of our lives.

Mr. Benjamin Bradshaw, London City Missionary,
sent me an interesting letter relating to some of these
sketches. It is as follows :—

"I thank you so much for sending letter and the
type-written papers, the reading of which I enjoyed
very much. It brought back to my heart old
memories of M'Cheyne. I read his memoir in 1883,
and can well call to mind the blessed peace it gave
me, and the strong desire to follow him as he followed
Christ. How very near he lived to his Master. He
must have known secrets that others, walking afar
off, never get revealed to them—yes, he must have
been a *Friend* of the Master's. "Henceforth I call
you not Servants but Friends, for all things I have
heard of my Father I have made known unto you"

(substance, John xv. 15). Lord, make us Friends, that we may know the Father's mind.

"Well, dear brother, I wish you every blessing in your blessed work for our Master. I enjoy very much the *Soul Winner*, which I get mostly every month. Some day I must write you out another little testimony. I herewith return your papers, and pray God's blessing on your new effort.

"I have been far from well for more than a week, but I am in the Master's hand.

> "Ill that He blesses is my good,
>   And unblest good is ill,
>   And all is right that seems most wrong,
>   If it be His sweet will."

And I have a note from a real poetess, Miss Lucy A. Bennett, who says: "I am a great admirer of R. M. M'Cheyne, and wish there were more of his apostolic succession. What a pleasure the remembrance must be to you!"

Then good old Rev. John Macpherson, late of Hilltown, Dundee, has a word for these revival incidents. As we mostly know, he has been in that glorious work himself for a generation or two, when it was said at one time during the revival of 1859, that perhaps a thousand anxious souls would visit him for instruction and spiritual help in the course of a year, and he has been a very valuable friend to me. "Many thanks," he writes, "for the enclosed sketch, No. 18. May the reading of these interesting details be blessed to many. I am truly glad that you are holding on so well in the good work given you to do.   My favourite text is, 'Jesus Christ, the same yesterday, and to-day, and for ever' (Heb. xiii. 8).—With warmest regards, yours sincerely, JOHN MACPHERSON."

And from Mrs. M. D. Manson, Edinburgh, a returned Calabar missionary, the following beautiful note was received, encouraging us to long and pray for times of revival to come again:—" Many thanks for sending me the sketch of the days of Robert Murray M'Cheyne, No. 16.   It is most interesting, and must recall most vividly to your mind the days when you were privileged to be acquainted with one so devoted and so fully blessed by the Master.   One is apt to look back upon such times of blessing as past and gone.   But do you not think that there are already signs of a revival on every hand, which may well eclipse anything that has yet been seen in our land?   The Lord hasten it in His own good time, and that He will grant us the privilege of being sharers therein.—I remain, yours in Him, M. D. MANSON."

And lastly (from friends) I give a few words from Mr. Arthur Y. Steel, missionary, Aden, on a visit home at present, who also expresses the longings of his heart for times of blessing to be granted us once more :—" I herewith return the two articles (Nos. 17 and 18) regarding the revivals under M'Cheyne, and have read them with much interest.   It makes one long more than ever for a great movement of the Holy Spirit throughout our land, and the ingathering of souls."

"I believe it to be the mind of Christ," Mr.

M'Cheyne wrote regarding *the Communion of the Lord's Supper*," that all who are vitally united to Him should love one another, exhort one another daily, communicate freely of their substances to one another when, poor, pray with and for one another, and sit down together at the Lord's table."—*Memoir and Remains*, p. 606. " The same blood has washed us, the same Spirit has quickened us; we lean upon the same pierced breast, we love the same Lord: we are guided by the same sleepless eye; we are to stand at the right hand of the same throne; we shall blend our voices eternally in singing the same song—Worthy is the Lamb!"

" I was once permitted to unite in celebrating the Lord's Supper in an upper room in Jerusalem. There were fourteen present, the most of whom, I had good reason to believe, knew and loved the Lord Jesus Christ. The bread and wine were dispensed in the Episcopal manner, and most were kneeling as they received them. We felt it to be sweet fellowship with Christ and with the brethren, and as we left the upper room, and looked out upon the Mount of Olives, we remembered with calm joy the prayer of our Lord that ascended from one of its shady ravines after the first Lord's Supper, ' Neither pray I for these alone, but for them also which still believe in Me through their word that they all may be one.'"—*Memoir and Remains*, p. 607.

" The table of Christ is a family table, spread in the wilderness, and none of the true children should be absent from it, or be separated while sitting at it.

"The Westminster Divines laid down the same principle in few but solemn words :—'Saints by profession are bound to maintain an holy fellowship and communion in the worship of God ; which communion as God offereth opportunity is to be extended unto all those who in every place call upon the name of the Lord Jesus.'—*Memoir and Remains*, p. 607.

In later days, during a sweet and gracious revival time, some young lads came and asked me to have meetings with them in dear Free St. David's, so we would meet in the Library and sing and pray and call on God together, and had real lovely times. There are only two or three of these dear young people to the fore now, but the memory of these days is still very sweet to my heart.

Mr. Thomas Kyd of Aberdeen has been interested in my sketches. He says : "Writing from the heart always tells. I am too young to remember M'Cheyne, who died when I was three. But I remember *Another Lily Gathered*, a story of James Laing, which my parents gave me when I was a child. And I have often looked at his portrait with his signature, "Ever yours till glory," as it appears in his biography. (Signed) THOMAS KYD."

So very many have got blessing from reading M'Cheyne's *Memoir and Remains*, by Dr. Andrew Bonar.

But ah ! there are calls for you and me, reader, to mourn over personal defections and falls ; yet, praise the Lord, the blood of Jesus applied can wash all these vile stains away.

> " Redemption, O wonderful story!
>   Glad message for you and for me,
> That Jesus has purchased our pardon,
>   And paid all the debt on the tree.

> " Accept now God's offer of mercy:
>   To Jesus, O hasten to-day!
> For He will receive him that cometh,
>   And never will turn him away.

> " Believe it, O sinner, believe it,
>   Receive the glad message—'tis true;
> Trust now in the crucified Saviour,
>   Salvation He offers to you."—S. M. SAYFORD.

I often go to Dundee Constitution Road graveyard for prayer and thanksgiving, and I have often noticed the great space on the south side of it, as it is quite bare. No funerals take place there, because during the cholera in these early days the dead bodies were piled in there, hundreds, or perhaps thousands, and an old man was lately telling what a dreadful sight it was. Perhaps the remembrance of this deplorable cholera scourge in these early days had left a solemn impression on many minds, for the last enemy then suddenly snatched many a one with ruthless violence away to the grave. I remember very well how we children used to stand and see the men with great blazing torches, which were carried about the streets with a view to burn up the foul infection in the air. These torches would be set down here and there leaning on some stone wall, perhaps, to let the bearers of them rest a little, and we would look on with astonishment, perhaps, or awe, at the unusual sights. I have a dim recollection, when I was a child, of my mother entering the room one morning, where I was under charge of her sister, and hearing exclamations of sorrow and surprise from her, as she was informed that my guardian, with whom I slept, was just then seized with the cholera, and in a short time passed away into eternity and was carried to her grave. Eternity! eternity! where will you be throughout eternity? Could I lift the thin veil which screens us from getting a view into eternity, how very solemnising it would be to see in a moment the glories of eternity. There we would see Jesus and the redeemed of God all casting their crowns at His feet.

> " Worthy the Lamb that died, they cry,
>   To be exalted thus ;
>   Worthy the Lamb, let us reply,
>   For He was slain for us."
>
> *Paraphrase* lxv. 6.

" I have seen many of the awakened persons," wrote Mr. M'Cheyne on 2nd December 1839, "and many of the saved. I find some old people deeply shaken ; they feel insecure. One confirmed drunkard has come to me, and is, I believe, now a saved man. Some little children are evidently saved. One convert of eleven years old is a singular instance of Divine grace. When I asked if she desired to be made holy, she said, " Indeed, I often wish I was awa' (away) that I might sin nae mair." A. S., of fifteen, is a fine, tender-hearted believer.   W. S., ten, is also a happy boy."—*Memoir*, p. 122.

In these old days, numbers of aged dames would sit on the pulpit stairs, and sometimes be pretty close up to the minister.   At times you might see some aged grannie on the pulpit stairs of churches, with a red cloth over her shoulders, quaint enough, and I think with a cap on her head instead of a bonnet.   Just think of the dear old lady getting up in the morning, having her early prayers for the Lord's choicest blessing on the work of the day, and then starting off for the house of God to hear Mr. M'Cheyne and the glorious gospel of salvation.   She might be coming along the old Kirk road, to be early in her place, her heart filled with Divine peace, and her lips whispering praise as God was with her by the way, upholding and blessing her.

> The auld Kirk road, the auld Kirk road,
> Where Grannie aften met wi' God ;
> She hirpled yont on Sabbath morn,
> For years afore that I was born.
>
> Her bonnet—na, it was a cap,
> That whiles her dear, neat pow wad hap ;
> An' aft the blast blew snell and cauld
> Aboot her heid, sae grey an' auld.
>
> Aneath her oxter was the Book,
> While faithfu' to the Kirk she took ;
> For Grannie read, an' Grannie sang,
> An' aft frae her God's praises rang.
>
> An' then, a'e Sabbath, white wi' snaw,
> Auld Grannie gently passed awa'.
> She trusted in her Saviour, God,
> An left for aye the auld Kirk road.

I have been visiting dear old Mrs. Wanless in Newport, and found her very frail. She loves to tell about Mr. M'Cheyne, and her conversion in these early days, and that the Lord is with her still. I gave her a little bag of scent, with the text on it, "Casting all your care upon Him, for He careth for you" (1 Pet. v. 7). She said—"I have had that text with me ever since I was a girl. I am eighty-four in February—next month. I joined the church in 1840, so I may say I was like Samuel, I have known the Lord since my youth." She learned a nice hymn at that time. I never heard it before. "I found it in my grandmother's trunk," she said. I asked her to repeat it, and I wrote it as she spoke, slowly:

> " I love the sacred Book of God,
>   None other can its place supply ;
>   It points me to the saints' abode,
>   It gives me wings and bids me fly.
>
> " Sweet Book, in thee mine eyes discern
>   The image of my absent Lord.
>   From thine instructive page I learn
>   The joy His presence will afford.
>
> " In thee I read my title clear
>   To mansions that will ne'er decay ;
>   My Lord ! O when shall He appear?
>   And bear His prisoner far away.
>
>   Then will I need thy Light no more,
>   For nothing shall be then concealed,
>   When I have reached the heavenly shore,
>   The Lord Himself will stand revealed.
>
>   But while I'm here, thou wilt supply
>   His place ; and tell me of His love.
>   I'd read with faith's discerning eye,
>   And get a taste of joys above.

" I know His Spirit breathes in thee,
  To animate His people here.
  May Thy sweet truths prove Life to me,
  Till in His presence I appear."

She gave me a message to the reader, namely—
" The Lord has kept me in the road, and led me and
guided me since I was young, and been kind to
me, and I have seen His providence in everything."
Then she continued—" I was very earnest for the
Sabbath; and if I had gone into a house on the
Sabbath day, and they had been speaking about
worldly things, I would have knelt down and prayed
for them. At one time I was coming home from a
meeting at twelve o'clock at night. It was held by
Rev. W. C. Burns, for we sometimes would be up to
one o'clock in the morning at the meetings. There
was no Forbes MacKenzie law at that time (when
publicans had to close their shops early). A man
came to me and said, ' Will you have a drink?' I
said yes, but you and I drink different water. I
drink "The Water of Life," holding up my Bible.
Then I gave him an awful hearing for attempting to
decoy young girls. Well, next night, he was in the
front of the gallery, hearing the Gospel. We had
a little prayer-meeting in Watt Street, Hawkhill,
Dundee, about six of us. We read and prayed and
sang psalms—it was not hymns at that time. Mr.
M‘Cheyne came occasionally to see how we conducted it.

" He got one of us to pray; then he prayed after
us; and seemed to approve of all we had prayed for.

" I am wearying to get away; but the Lord is

getting something for me to do : I have been able to help some things.   But we cannot be long now." I repeated part of the 37th Psalm and prayed.   She said, " When I waken at night I get some comforting passages—' Fear not, for I have redeemed thee.   I have called thee by thy name ; thou art Mine ' (Isa. xliii. 1).   Mrs. J. L., Newport (a kind lady), pays one pound a week for a night-nurse for me.   My room on Sabbath is kept like a prayer-meeting, with visits from friends."

So ended my interesting visit to dear Mr. M'Cheyne's old " Young Convert."

XX

MANY people have written about home as being the dearest spot on earth to them. But we can be fairly allowed to consider our church as also a very dear place. Perhaps where we were baptized, where we so long sat with our dear parents and friends and children; where we gave our hearts to the Lord under the sound of the blessed Gospel of salvation, and where we humbly sought to serve the dear Redeemer who died for us, there must be attraction there! They would be cold and unsympathetic who had not fragrant memories of the loved ones who have long since left these pews and us, for the Better Land on high. But when added to this the pastor is of the true type, and greatly endears himself by his pure, holy, Scriptural preaching, and most of all by his beautiful, gracious life, then we can say our church vies with our home, for it is there where we have comfort and peace and joy. One dear old friend of mine said, "I have only my church and my churchyard now."

I have heard that very many strangers from a distance, or from other lands, make it a point to visit St. Peter's Church, where Mr. M'Cheyne preached, early on their arrival in Dundee, and perhaps stand in the pulpit where this man of God proclaimed the glorious Gospel of the blessed God to the gathered, earnest crowds around.   Here or at the Communion table one day he cried out—" Ah, Judas! I know you. You will betray me." Again, in a very searching sermon, marked Dundee, 1836, he concluded as follows : " Oh, what a wonderful thing the eye of faith is !   It sees beyond the stars, it pierces to the throne of God, and there it looks on the face of Jesus, making intercession for us, "Whom having not seen, we love; in whom, though now we see Him not, yet, believing, we rejoice with joy unspeakable and full of glory."   Oh, if you would live thus, what sweet peace would fill your bosom ! and how many droppings of the Spirit would come down on you in answer to the Saviour's prayer ! Oh, how your face would shine like Stephen's, and the poor blind world would see that there is a joy which the world cannot take away—a heaven upon earth." And, lastly, his sermon on Heb. ii. 16–18: " For verily He took not on Him the nature of angels, but He took on Him the seed of Abraham.   Wherefore in all things it behoved Him to be made like unto His brethren, that He might be a merciful and faithful High Priest in things pertaining to God, to make reconciliation for the sins of the people.   For in that He Himself hath suffered being tempted, He is able to succour them that are tempted." " Ah, believers, you are a tempted people ! You are always poor and needy, and God intends it should be so, to give you constant errands to go to Jesus. His work was not all done on Calvary. He that died for our sins lives to pray for us, to help in every time of need. He is

still man on the right hand of God.   He is still God,
and therefore by reason of His divinity is present
here this day as much as any of us.   He knows your
every sorrow, trial, and difficulty—every half-hearted
sigh.   He hears and brings in notice thereof to
His human heart at the right hand of God.   His
human heart is the same yesterday and to-day and
for ever.   It pleads for you, thinks on you, plans
deliverance for you.   Dear tempted brethren! go
boldly to the throne of grace to obtain mercy, and
find grace to help you in your time of need.   Are
you bereaved of one you loved?   Go and tell Jesus.
Spread out your sorrows at His feet.   He knows
them all, feels for you in them all.   He is a merciful
High Priest.   He is faithful, too, never awanting in
the hour of need.   He is able to succour you by His
Word, by His Spirit, by His providence.   He gave you
all the comfort you had by your friends.   He can
give it you without them.   He has taken away the
stream that you may go to the fountain.   Are you
suffering in body?   Go to this High Priest.   He is
intimately acquainted with all your diseases.   He has
felt that very pain.   Remember how, when they brought
to Him one that was deaf and had an impediment in
his speech, He looked up to heaven and sighed, and
said Ephphatha.   He sighed over his misery (as if
he felt it), so He sighs over you.   He is able to give
you deliverance, or patience to bear it, or improvement
by it.   Are you sore tempted in soul, put into trying
circumstances, so that you know not what to do?
Look up, He is able to succour you.   If He had been
on earth, would you not have gone to Him?—would

you not have knelt and said, 'Lord, help me'?
Does it make any difference that He is at the right
hand of God? He is the same yesterday, and to-
day, and for ever" (see *Memoir and Remains*). But
many friends of Mr. M'Cheyne may never get to
Dundee to see his pulpit in his own church of St.
Peter's, so I have just got it specially photographed.

Miss M. Sime, Dundee, who was a young convert
under Mr. M'Cheyne, has just written me the following nice note, as she returned my last sketch, No. 19,
in which I gave the names of the ministers who used
to meet together in Dundee for prayer on Monday,
after the work of the Sabbath day. " Many thanks,"
she writes, "for the reading of another sketch about
M'Cheyne and others. It is very interesting to me.
I feel very much refreshed by reading over the names
of those dear ministers who met for prayer in those
days, as I have heard the most of them preach.
And also about Mr. Riddell of Glasgow (my old
minister), and others, who are meeting for the same
purpose in Glasgow. I do hope and pray that some
of our Dundee ministers would be stirred up to meet
together for prayer, that the blessed work of revival
may come speedily to our city. May the Lord lay
it on their hearts. The Lord bless you in your work
more and more is the prayer of your friend in Jesus.
—M. Sime."

Perhaps when this lady gave her heart to Jesus in
1839, or so, some friend may have said, "Will she
hold out?" Praise God, this artless letter from her
may be called an undesigned coincidence or testimony

that in all these long years she is still able to say,
"Trusting in Jesus, I know I am blessed."

Just about this time in my writing I have been
hearing of the death and funeral of my old friend
and distant relative, Bailie Macdonald of Dundee,
who got several of these sketches to read, which he
said he handed to his minister, the Rev. Mr. White,
now the minister of St. Peter's. Mr. Macdonald was
session-clerk in that church for some fifty years, and
I am told by a friend of his to-day that Mr. and Mrs.
Macdonald were the last two of his congregation
whom M'Cheyne married before his death.

Another old lady friend of mine, Mrs. Dewar, writes
me that she was in the church that night Mr. M'Cheyne
came home from the Holy Land. It was on a
Thursday evening, for I was present myself and
heard his address. It was expected that he would
give an account of his travels, but he gave out
Ps. lxvi. :

> "All lands to God, in joyful sounds,
>   Aloft your voices raise,
> Sing forth the honour of His name,
>   And glorious make His praise.
> Say unto God, How terrible
>   In all Thy works art Thou !
> Through Thy great pow'r Thy foes to The
>   Shall be constrain'd to bow.
>
> "All on the earth shall worship Thee,
>   They shall Thy praise proclaim,
> In songs they shall sing cheerfully
>   Unto Thy holy name.
> Come, and the works that God hath wrought
>   With admiration see :
> In's working to the sons of men
>   Most terrible is He."

After solemn prayer, he was able to preach for about an hour from I Cor. ii. 1–4 : " And I, brethren, when I came to you, came not with the excellency of speech, or of wisdom, declaring unto you the testimony of God. For I determined not to know anything among you, save Jesus Christ, and Him crucified. And I was with you in weakness, and in fear, and in much trembling. And my speech and my preaching was not with enticing words of man's wisdom, but in demonstration of the Spirit and of power."

On coming out of the church, he found the road to his house crowded with old and young, who were waiting to welcome him back. He had to shake hands with many at the same time, and before this happy multitude would disperse had to speak some words of life to them again, and pray with them where they stood. " To Thy name, O Lord," said he, that night when he returned to his home,—" To Thy name, O Lord, be all the glory."

On Sabbath, after his return from his travels, he preached to his flock in the afternoon from 2 Chron. v. 13, 14 : " It came even to pass, as the trumpeters and singers were as one, to make one sound to be heard in praising and thanking the Lord ; and when they lifted up their voice with the trumpets, and cymbals, and instruments of music, and praised the Lord, saying, For He is good ; for His mercy endureth for ever ; that then the house was filled with a cloud, even the house of the Lord : so that the priests could not stand to minister by reason of the cloud ; for the glory of the Lord had filled the house of God."   In closing, his hearers remember

well how affectionately and solemnly he said:
"Dearly beloved and longed for, I now begin another
year of my ministry among you, and I am resolved,
if God give me health and strength, that I will not
let a man, woman, or child among you alone, until
you have at least heard the testimony of God concerning His Son, either to your condemnation or
salvation. And I will pray as I have done before,
that if the Lord will indeed give us a great outpouring
of His Spirit, He will do it in such a way that it
will be evident to the weakest child among you that
it is the Lord's work and not man's. I think I may
say to you, as Rutherford said to his people, 'Your
heaven would be two heavens to me.' And if the
Lord be pleased to give me a crown from among
you, I do here promise in His sight that I will cast
it at His feet, saying, 'Worthy is the Lamb that was
slain. Blessing and honour and glory and power be
unto Him that sitteth upon the throne, and unto the
Lamb for ever and ever'" (Rev. v. 12, 13).

My aged friend Mrs. Dewar, in her letter to me,
also says: "I can hear the bell tolling on his funeral
day. When I think of all the happy days," she continued, "I have spent about St. Peter's, I can only
say, 'Oh, that He would rend the heavens and come
down, as in the days of a Communion season.' We
would be along at the church at ten o'clock, and
never out till five in the afternoon, and sorry to
leave. Now I must stop, for I could go on speaking
about all the blessed times that I like to think upon."

The old bells of St. Peter's Church (to which Mrs.
Dewar refers) in these early days had a solemn chime

as they would sound out on the holy Sabbath day,
or for the great meetings perhaps night after night.
And I may mention here, that no bells I ever heard
had such beauty in their tones and solemnity in their
associations as these.   I have heard bells on the great
St. Isaac's Cathedral in St. Petersburg, Russia; on
St. Giles', Cripplegate, London, where John Milton
is buried (very beautiful); in Norway, when we were
called to pray for peace, when the Swedish flag was
pulled down; also the clanging bell of our steamer in
the fog on the Atlantic, as for some hundreds of
miles we sailed cautiously along, the outlook calling
aloud every few minutes, "All's well, and the lights
are burning brightly, sir."   But no bells were so
beautiful, even affecting to hear, as the old bells of
St. Peter's, and the people would assemble at their
call, some perhaps with hearts filled with sorrow for
sin, or anxiety for their eternal welfare, or glad in
the joy and peace of believing, with all sin and sorrow
washed away in the precious, atoning, peace-speaking
blood of the Lamb.

Mrs. Dewar enclosed in one of her letters to me the
following printed verses, which well deserve a place in
this article :—

A LITTLE WHILE.

"Only a little while of brave endeavour,
  Only a little while of care and strife,
And then—the perfect peace of God for ever,
  And the pure glories of the fadeless life.

"Only a little while of patient yearning
  For vanished smiles, and voices hushed of yore,
And then—our loved ones with their Lord returning,
  And hands now severed, clasped to part no more.

"O blissful day! O glorious consummation!
   Lo, o'er the hills the dawn is breaking fast!
Come, Light of life, display Thy full salvation,
   And speed the lowly pilgrim home at last."—S. C. LOWRY.

At this point I hear of the death of Mr. Ira D. Sankey, the great and sweet singer of the songs of the Gospel. One warrior after another is falling in the fight. May the good Lord raise up others, willing and brave and true, for the great battle now being urged in these latter days for the Lord Jesus and His Word, His atonement and His crown.

"Not all the blood of beasts,
   On Jewish altars slain,
Could give the guilty conscience peace,
   Or wash away the stain.

"But Christ, the heavenly Lamb,
   Takes all our sins away,
A sacrifice of nobler name
   And richer blood than they.

"My faith would lay her hand
   On that dear head of Thine,
While like a penitent I stand,
   And there confess my sin.

"My soul looks back to see
   The burden Thou did'st bear
When hanging on th' accursed tree,
   And knows her guilt was there."—ISAAC WATTS.

It is possible that Mr. Sankey had sung in St. Peter's Church, for I know that Mr. Moody preached there one day, and had the joy of pointing a young Dundee lady, as she stood in anxiety of soul to find the Lord at Mr. M‘Cheyne's grave, to the Lamb of God who taketh away the sins of the world, and she went on her way rejoicing. And I well recollect how my son and I crossed the great Brooklyn bridge in search of Mr. Sankey's house; but, behold, he was away on a visit to Mr. Moody at Northfield, or other-where, and we did not meet the dear man. "Jesus of Nazareth passeth by," "Dare to be a Daniel," "I am so glad that our Father in Heaven," "The Ninety and Nine," and "Rescue the Perishing," will be lasting memorials of the great mission singer, Ira D. Sankey. The first time I heard Mr. Sankey was in Free St. Andrew's Church, Dundee, as he came in while the people were assembling, and, I think, sang the fine hymn—

> "Sweet hour of prayer, sweet hour of prayer,
> That calls me from a world of care,
> And bids me at my Father's throne
> Make all my wants and wishes known."

And in Moody and Sankey's last meeting in Dundee, again held in St. Andrew's Church, I had the pleasure of being the last speaker, as I then thanked Mr. Sankey for teaching us the power of sacred song.

And I have a kind note from Rev. Mr. Shaw, the pastor of St. Andrew's Church, in which he says: "Many thanks for the enclosed sketch, No. 16, which I now return. I like that sentence of yours about the revived believer's actings—'Even the heathen feel and participate in the wave of heavenly power, as his prayers and his means float along to distant shores.' Mr. M‘Cheyne's kindness to the poor serving girl is very touching.—Yours very truly, CHARLES SHAW." (See page 171.)

Mrs. David M. M'Intyre of Glasgow kindly writes me, thanking me for a reading of sketch No. 19, and says: "I have a Bible he liked to use, with notes in his (Mr. M'Cheyne's) own handwriting.

"You may be interested in the copy of one or two of these that I enclose now.

"*Psalm* xlix. 4.   Ministers must first incline their ear to hear what God will say, then they may open the hidden things of God to their people.

"He must be first in the counsel of God, etc.

"*Psalm* xxii.   May my eyes be opened to see wonders out of this psalm.

"1. May I see the infinite compassion of Father, Son, and Holy Ghost, in giving up a Divine Person to be a worm and no man.

"2. May I see the infinite vileness of sinners, that such sufferings needed to be borne—how much my sin must be.

"3. May I see what Faith is in darkness: my God, my God !

"4. May I see how free Christ is, and I in Him, from any more wrath.

"5. May I see the awful nature of the sin of un-belief.   How shall we escape if we neglect so great Salvation.

"*Psalm* xxxii. 1.   Paul tells us (in Rom. iv. 6) that David speaks here of the blessedness of the justified man, the man who is righteous without works, through the imputed righteousness of Christ.

"But as David is speaking with regard to a particular

occasion, when he peculiarly found this blessedness, he adds, verse second—'*in whose spirit there is no guile.*' That is, who goes simply to God for his righteousness.

" David seems to have been a believer, under guilt of some recent sin, and the guile spoken of is the guile of keeping back from Christ—under the idea that we are not ready to go to Him, having sinned against His light and against His blood."

My good friend, Mr. Henry S. Deas of Forfar, writes a few kindly words, as follows:—" Anything and everything about M'Cheyne has had a great fascination for me. Ever since I first read his *Memoir*, by Dr. Bonar, many years ago when quite a lad, the work and life of M'Cheyne has been quite an inspiration to me as to many others, and your nice articles will recall to many the upward feelings that the hope of revival ever gives us, will stimulate us all to more earnest prayer that we may soon have such glorious times again.

" Behold the Lord's hand is not shortened that it cannot save, neither is His ear heavy that it cannot hear (Isa. lix. 1).

" The fault must be ours, for hath He not said: ' For this shall I be enquired of by the house of Israel to do it for them.'

" Yea He would have us give Him no rest until He make bare His arm, and vindicate His name and glorious Gospel.

" Let us continue to plead that the Word of God may have free course and be glorified, as it used to be in Pentecostal times, or in 1859 and 1860, or in Moody and Sankey, and Torry and Alexander's times.—Believe me, yours sincerely in the bonds of the Gospel of our Lord Jesus Christ, HENRY S. DEAS.

XXI

THERE seems to have been means used by Mr. M'Cheyne for the noble, even glorious, times which were seen in his short but brief life on earth. Like Frances Ridley Havergal, who wished to cram in all she possibly could for the Lord Jesus while life was granted to her, so I will give the gentle reader a peep behind the scenes in the daily round of Robert Murray M'Cheyne's life. May it be as an example to the believers, especially to ministers and to us all.

"I am persuaded," he wrote, "that I shall obtain the highest amount of present happiness; I shall do most for God's glory and the good of man, and I shall have the fullest reward in eternity, by maintaining a conscience always washed in Christ's blood; by being filled with the Holy Spirit at all times, and by attaining the most entire likeness to Christ, in mind, will, and heart that is possible for a redeemed sinner to attain to in this world."—*Memoir*, p. 155.

"As I was walking in the field," he again wrote, "the thought came over me with overwhelming power, that every one of my flock must soon be in heaven or hell. Oh, how I wished that I had a tongue like thunder that I might make all hear it, or that I had a frame like iron, that I might visit every one and say, 'Escape for thy life.'"

"It is the duty of ministers," he continues, "in this day to begin the reformation of religion and manners with themselves, families, etc., with confession of past sin, earnest prayer for direction, grace, and full purpose of heart. 'He shall purify the sons of Levi' (Mal. iii. 3). Ministers are probably laid aside for a time for this very purpose. Often when I sleep long, or meet with others early and then have family prayer and breakfast and forenoon callers, often it is eleven or twelve o'clock before I begin secret prayer. This is a wretched system. It is unscriptural. Christ rose before day and went into a solitary place. David says, 'Early will I seek Thee.' Mary Magdalene came to the sepulchre while yet it was dark. I ought to spend the best hours of the day in communion with God. It is my noblest and most fruitful employment, and is not to be thrust into a corner. The morning hours, from six to eight, are the most uninterrupted, and should be thus employed if I can prevent drowsiness. A little time after breakfast might be given to intercession. After tea is my best hour, and that should be solemnly dedicated to God if possible. I ought not to give up the good old habit of prayer before going to bed, but guard must be kept against sleep: planning what things I am to ask is the best remedy. When I awake in the night I ought to rise and pray, as David and John Welsh did. I ought to read three chapters of the Bible in secret every day at least. I should pray much more in peaceful days, that I may be guided rightly when days of trial come."—*Memoir*, p. 164.

From the above earnest exercises of the heart and

of the pen, I daresay my friends may candidly admit that it was likely God would very graciously command the blessing to fall upon and follow a minister like M'Cheyne, as he has written the following words in the Scriptures for the benefit and encouragement of such as live close to Him, whether minister or layman: "Call unto Me and I will answer thee, and show thee great and mighty things which thou knowest not" (Jer. xxxiii. 3).

If I might be allowed to testify humbly from my own experience, after I have had long seasons with the Lord, I would perhaps get very gracious answers to prayer, or power to love and serve Him more and more. And I think it is the Norwegians who have a saying that God does not require to search about for a person to do His special work, but just takes the one nearest at hand, who is living close to Him in love, and prayer, and faith, and obedience, or such like; therefore, let us all live very near to God so as to get His favour, His power, and His love.

I wish to show the reader a picture of Mr. M'Cheyne's manse, which I have had specially photographed. It is done just in time, as the building is now taken down to make more room in the manufacturing premises of the proprietor. One day some months ago I visited the dear old manse while it was still to the fore, in the west end of Dundee. I was in the study where Mr. M'Cheyne had composed many of his solemn words of warning, and many of his cheering and helpful and gracious words of comfort and peace. I stood in the chamber where the dear young minister died, and where he yielded up his immortal spirit to Him who gave it, and there, in affecting tones, I prayed a few sentences, but I dare say my words were few and faltering there that day.   Yes! it was solemn to visit the old manse, which will never be seen again but in picture form, as it is here to-day.   This was the chamber where he, at the first of this closing scene of his life, requested to be left alone for half an hour.   When his servant entered the room again, Mr. M'Cheyne exclaimed with a joyful voice, "My soul is escaped as a bird out of the snare of the fowler; the snare is broken, and I am escaped."—*Memoir*, p. 168.

But it might be well here to let other friends of M'Cheyne speak out their earnest, loving appreciation of his life and labours, which may be a confirmation of much of what I have written in these sketches, which numbers of my friends have read both at home and abroad.   Dear Dr. Andrew Bonar said: "There is still some peculiar fragrance in the air around Robert M'Cheyne's grave."

A domestic servant at Collace, where he often visited, said: "Oh, to hear Mr. M'Cheyne at prayer in the morning!   It was as if he would never give over, he had so much to ask.   You would have thought the very walls would speak again."

The Rev. John Roxburgh of Dundee wrote of Mr. M'Cheyne as follows (see *Memoir and Remains*): "Whether viewed as a son, a brother, a friend, or a pastor, often has the remark been made by those who knew him most intimately, that he was the most faultless and attractive exhibition of the true Christian which they had ever seen embodied in a living form."

Dear old Rev. John Baxter of Blairgowrie had also a good word for the young minister of St. Peter's. I say young minister, for the reader should know that he died in the thirtieth year of his age, and did all his great work before perhaps some ministers leave the college. " He was one of the most complete ministers I ever saw," said Mr. Baxter. " He was a great preacher, an excellent visitor, a full-orbed saint. He visited the dying on Saturdays, that his heart might be thrilled by what he saw, and that he might be put into an arrested and serious frame for Sabbath work."

Again, the Rev. K. Hewat, M.A., in writing a preface to *M'Cheyne from the Pew*, says: " That the religious public of Scotland and of other lands are still interested in the life and work of M'Cheyne is evident from the extensive sale which still goes on of Dr. Andrew Bonar's *Memoirs and Remains* of that saintly man. Since that book was first published, over 150,000 copies have been sold, in addition to 50,000 of the *Memoir* without the *Remains*, and it has been found in the most out-of-the-way farmhouses and shepherd huts of America and Australia. This little book," Mr. Hewat continues, " is not intended to supplement that religious classic, but just again to show forth the piety and zeal of a devoted minister of the Gospel."

The writer of this little book, referred to above, was an elder in St. Peter's Church, and on the third day of partaking of the Communion there he wrote: " How beautifully affectionate was Mr. M'Cheyne's address. He draws you to Christ. To-day he said,

'Christ has brought us into green pastures and by still waters, but would we follow the Shepherd into deep valleys of affliction and trial? Ah, true! it is easy to follow Christ when the way is smooth, but very difficult when the world, worldly desires, pursuits, and pleasures are in our way, as stones and traps which make us stumble. I felt composed and comforted, though downcast, because of my walking too much away from Christ.'" The dear man (Mr. Lamb) who wrote these words was thrown from his horse and killed. "The silver cord was loosed," his *Memoir* adds, "and the golden bowl was broken. All too early, at the age of thirty-three, he passed away. Yet in his comparatively short life he had lived much, allowing no talent to remain unused, and no opportunity of serving his Master, the Lord Jesus Christ, to pass away unimproved."

The Rev. Andrew Moody, D.D., Edinburgh, late of Budapest, some time ago, in acknowledging one of my sketches, wrote me: "It is wonderful how the record of M'Cheyne's life, and the revival in Dundee, has moved and still moves the hearts of many."

Lord Kinnaird of Rossie Priory wrote me from Geneva the following very sympathetic letter as to the work of revival in religion. Lord Kinnaird is the acting chairman of the Evangelical Alliance of Great Britain, and his words are entitled to have much weight with us all:—

"HOTEL DE LECIE, GENEVA.

"Many thanks for letting me see the enclosed cutting (No. 19), with reminiscences of the days of M'Cheyne. What a wonderful power there is in the influence of one man fully consecrated to God's service! I trust there are beginnings of indications in many quarters that God's people are longing for a revival, and that bands are praying that we may see multitudes converted, and then the results which followed M'Cheyne's preaching shall recur, bands of praying men and women and boys and girls. I do not think we must expect an exact copy of 1859 methods, for the Holy Spirit walks in divers ways. I trust that conferences at Perth and Dundee may be real times of blessing. We must unitedly pray for this.—Yours very truly,

"KINNAIRD."

I also received a very nice letter from Mr. James Logie, Dundee, saying that he had read my article (No. 17) with great interest and pleasure. "My earliest recollections," he says, "are associated with M'Cheyne. The letters of Bonar and M'Cheyne from the Holy Land appeared in the *United Secession Magazine*, and were read by us at home with very great interest and appreciation. I had the unspeakable advantage of being trained in a truly Christian home, for which I never cease to bless God, and these letters to which I refer show that we were brought to take a wide interest in the cause and kingdom of our Lord and Saviour. While one cannot but deplore the spirit of worldliness that still so largely prevails in the world, yet I cannot but feel that the Kingdom is growing, and my faith is strong enough to feel assured that He must reign till all His

enemies are subdued.   As in Adam all die, even so
in Christ shall all be made alive.   Christ came that
we might have life, and that we might have it more
abundantly, but this Kingdom of God is within us
by the indwelling of the Holy Spirit."   Mr. Logie has
since passed away to be for ever with the Lord.

Now comes my old and valued friend, the Rev.
George G. Cameron, D.D., Professor of Hebrew in
the University of Aberdeen.   He as minister and I
as session-clerk laboured in Free St. David's, Dundee,
together, long ago.   Now the dear old building is
abolished, and its story is common property to the
public :—

"ABERDEEN, 30*th December* 1907.

"MY DEAR MR. SMITH,—I am just home from
Dundee, where it was my melancholy duty to preach
the last sermon that will ever be preached in dear old
Free St. David's.   As it was the place where my first
sermon was preached as a probationer entering on
his work, the occasion was to me both solemn and
trying.   God grant that the evangelical spirit which
characterised the congregation in 1866 may be the
animating spirit in the congregation in its new sphere
of service, and that the new St. David's may not
merely continue but increase the success of old
St. David's, in all efforts that make for the conversion
of men to God, and the establishment of righteousness
in the earth.   I have read your articles with the
greatest interest.   Dr. Roxburgh, with whom I began
my ministry as colleague, used to tell me a good deal
about St. Peter's and M‘Cheyne, and apart from the
public material at the disposal of all regarding that

godly remarkable man, your report of his manner of
working is not merely worthy of record, but throws a
fresh light—the most interesting light of all, because
that of personal experience—on one of the most
remarkable spiritual movements that have found a
place in the religious life of Scotland. With all the
good wishes of the season to you and yours,—I am,
etc.,   GEO. G. CAMERON."

I will here give a kindly acceptable word from a
lady, wife of an ex-Provost, returning my sketch,
No. 20:—" Very beautiful!   I read it aloud to all the
family, and they were all delighted with it."

But I must call a halt from my many interesting
letters received, concluding with one from a minister
who occupied Mr. M'Cheyne's pulpit at one time, the
Rev. James Burnet, Lochee, as follows:—" I shall
ever regard it as a high privilege and a sacred
responsibility that for seven and a half months, from
June 1885 to February 1886, I was assistant to the
Rev. John Jenkins in St. Peter's Church, and frequently had the opportunity of preaching the Gospel
in M'Cheyne's pulpit.   How the atmosphere of that
remarkable man of God clings to the dear and sacred
place!   I think I can say it was a means of deepening
my own spiritual life, quickening my desire to work
for our glorious Master, and since returning to Dundee
(from the north) I have had opportunities of again
standing in dear M'Cheyne's pulpit and proclaiming
the Word of Life, and never without a sweet and
solemn consciousness of the holy influence of the
place.   Can it be otherwise to those who have read

the *Memoirs and Remains*, and have entered in any degree into the Christ-like spirit of Robert Murray M'Cheyne? But my connection with St. Peter's may be said to be hereditary as well as personal, for during Mr. M'Cheyne's ministry my maternal grandfather and grandmother, Mr. and Mrs. Thomas Davidson, were members of his church. Often have I heard my grandmother speak in glowing terms of M'Cheyne and the grand times of blessing in St. Peter's; and my own dear mother, who went home a few years ago, remembered distinctly of the man of God placing his hand on her head when playing in the vicinity of St. Peter's. Praying that you may be long spared, etc. etc., (Signed) JAMES BURNET."

May the aroma of these articles about dear, godly Robert Murray M'Cheyne be felt to have a sweet and gracious influence for God and for His glory. Our lives get better than ever, to be lived by us all for Him. The market to be purer; the home to be happier in the Lord; common life made sanctified and lovely, with the softer blue of heaven and the bright beyond in the distance. And may our everyday experience of sunshine and shadow be made about perfect by the sweet consciousness of our having Christ in our hearts the hope of glory.

Let us all pray that the glory of God may be sought in all the churches by pastors and people. Old Thomas Watson writes, about A.D. 1660, " Glorifying of God consists of four things :—

" *First.* Appreciation, to set God highest in our thoughts, Ps. xcii. 8, 'Thou Lord art most high for evermore.'

" *Second.* Adoration or worship, Ps. xxix. 2, ' Give unto the Lord the glory due unto His name ; worship the Lord in the beauty of Holiness.'

" *Third.* Affection, God counts Himself glorified when He is loved. 'Thou shalt love the Lord thy God with all thy heart, and with all thy soul, and with all thy strength.'

" *Fourth.* Subjection, when we dedicate ourselves to God, and stand ready dressed for His service. Thus you see wherein glorifying God doth consist, in appreciation, adoration, affection, and subjection."

XXII

MUCH more might be said of dear Mr. M'Cheyne; but I now conclude these chapters, trusting the Lord will accompany their publication with His divine blessing. I will ask the reader's kind forbearance, as they have been written at intervals of some years.

"How much is there contained in a living man of the study of God, the genius of God, the poetry of God? My trembling and agitated breast frequently pants after leisure to look into the revelation of God" (M. Tyrius).

As we walk round a garden and mark the beautiful colouring of the different flowers, so we can move in the world, and marvel at the various habits and characteristics of the people whom we meet. And when a M'Cheyne is seen or heard or studied, there is an outstanding and lasting impression which comes to our spirit, because we know that by such contact with grace, the fragrance of heaven is upon us, inspiring us with holy memories, sympathies, and aspirations.

But though unheard or unseen by the reader, a few dim glimpses of this man of God may have been presented in these pages, and be interesting. May the lessons from his young, and active, and holy life

and death be useful to some of this new generation,
from that in which he preached and laboured and
prayed. And may the fruit of this humble effort be
for the glory of God, and be greatly blessed by Him
to readers, so that we may all have a happy meeting
in eternity.

I will now have the pleasure to give the reader a
beautiful account of dear Mr. M'Cheyne to me from
the pen of my friend, the Rev. William Milne of
Montreux, Switzerland. We had a very delightful
visit to his home some years ago. "I thank you,"
he writes me, "for a reading of your paper on
M'Cheyne and his times. You do well to keep his
name before this generation. There is life in his
bones, as there was in the prophet's of old. His
Memoir by dear Andrew Bonar is still a life-giving
book. I gave a copy of it to a French lady last week.
She was very pleased to get it.

"I have a vivid recollection of Mr. M'Cheyne.
I heard him speak at a meeting on the Church crisis
in 1842. He rose up so quick after a stirring speech
by Mr. or Dr. Alexander of Kirkcaldy, and said,
'They want us to take Christ's crown from His royal
brow and place it upon Cæsar; but that is what *we
will not do.*'

"These words were uttered with such a spirit of
quick determination, that they made a deep impression. They seemed to sum up the whole argument
against Erastianism, and for spiritual independence.
I also heard him preach in the Church of Cruden,
on Paul as a pattern to all who should believe.
I could never forget the solemnity of the appeal at

the close of the sermon. He used words to this effect:
'We may not meet again till we stand before God at
the judgment day; and if any of you are not saved,
you will have no excuse. Paul was saved as a
pattern, and I have set him before you as a
pattern, and if you are not saved, Paul will
be there to condemn you; and *I will be there to
condemn you.*'

"And with these words, pronounced in a quick but
awfully solemn manner, he closed the Bible. That
sermon made a very deep impression on more than me.
I heard him also give an address to the parents of a
child whom he baptized at Hatton, in Cruden. I do
not remember anything he said, except that he spoke
about the necessity of being born again; but what
impressed me on that occasion, as I looked at him,
was the expression of *his eyes*. I thought I had never
seen such eyes. They seemed to me to glow with
supernatural fire, and I quite sympathised with the
remark of a farmer, who was himself a godless man,
when he said, 'If ever God dwelt in any man, He is
in *that man.*'

"These are my reminiscences of Robert Murray
M'Cheyne. They are living and vivid to-day after
sixty-six years.—Ever yours in the blessed hope,
W. MILNE."

The Rev. Mr. Sutherland, of the M'Cheyne
Memorial Church, Dundee, sends me a very nice
note as follows:—

"In the vestry of my church there lies a Bible
with this inscription: 'Presented to the Rev. Robert
Murray M'Cheyne, minister of St. Peter's Church,

Dundee, by the members of his congregation, as a mark of their affection and esteem. January 1837. 2 Thess. i. 11, 12.'

"This Bible bears marks of frequent perusal, especially at the 'Song of Solomon,' a book from which the preacher drew many of his most spiritual addresses.

"M'Cheyne's memory lives on and his influence abides in the lives of the now rapidly diminishing number of those who knew him personally, and caught the fire of his great passion for souls.

"M'Cheyne's *Lord* still lives, and is able and willing to give, in answer to believing prayer, spiritual quickening such as that enjoyed in those early days of revival, and so much needed by the Church of to-day.—ANDREW N. SUTHERLAND, M.A., Minister of M'Cheyne's Memorial United Free Church, Dundee."

Mr. Sutherland continues:

"I add here the portion of his Bible which bears special marks, from the following verses:

Song of Solomon, chap. i. 12, "While the King sitteth at his table, my spikenard sendeth forth the smell thereof."

Chap. ii. 3. "I sat down under his shadow with great delight, and his fruit was sweet to my taste."

Chap. ii. 16. "My beloved is mine, and I am His."

Chap. iii. 4. "Him whom my soul loveth."

M'Cheyne could say, like Paul, "To me to live is Christ."

The late Rev. T. S. Dickson of Edinburgh wrote

me, dear man of God, some time before his death. He was great on our giving a stated portion of our means to the Lord. I am pleased to say I do so, and "The Lord's Book" is kept with debtor and creditor sides. The reader should adopt this good plan. Even the heathen gave their tenths to the Temple.

And you remember what Jacob said, "This stone which I have set for a pillar shall be God's house, and of all that Thou shalt give me, I will surely give the tenth unto Thee (Gen. xxviii. 22). And the Apostle Paul says, in 1 Cor. xvi. 2, "Upon the first day of the week let every one of you lay by him in store as God hath prospered him." "My dear friend," wrote Mr. Dickson to me (without date), "your reminiscences of M'Cheyne and his times are full of interest to me, who spent ten years of my ministerial life in Dundee, and often passed his church and tombstone. Times are greatly changed since M'Cheyne's day, and there is less desire for the preached Word.

"God will doubtless raise up preachers suited to preach the unchanging Gospel to the changed times. For amidst all the wonderful changes, the needs of human nature are the same. The opening verses in Ps. xxxvii. are very often on my mind, and I often quote them in speech and letter.—Yours in our Master's service, T. S. DICKSON.

PSALM XXXVII.

"For evil doers fret thou not
    Thyself unquietly;
Nor do thou envy bear to those
    That work iniquity.

"For even like unto the grass,
    Soon be cut down shall they;
And like the green and tender herb,
    They wither shall away.

"Set thou thy trust upon the Lord,
    And be thou doing good;
And so thou in the land shalt dwell,
    And verily have food.

"Delight thyself in God, He'll give
    Thine heart's desire to thee.
Thy way to God commit, Him trust,
    It bring to pass shall He.

"And, like unto the light, He shall
    Thy righteousness display;
And He thy judgment shall bring forth
    Like noontide of the day.

"Rest in the Lord, and patiently
    Wait for Him, do not fret
For him who, prospering in his way,
    Success in sin doth get."

These verses have been favourites of mine also for many years.

At this stage I would like to say a word. I think on the nice text, "Redeeming the time, because the days are evil." In our short, brief lives, dear reader, let us be active. Christ *died* for us, surely we should do something for Him now! We are not to waste our time and strength on "trifles light as air."

Some years ago I read the life of Rev. Mr. Macphail of Resolis. When on his death-bed, he was one night peculiarly restless. His friends asked him the reason of his tossings to and fro upon his bed.

The memorable answer he gave was, "That he felt as much assured of being for ever with his Saviour as he was of lying on his bed; but I know not," said he, "how I can look Him in the face, when I think *how little I have done for Him.*"

O may we all be earnest in our lives, for the Lord Jesus Christ.   Amen.

Our aged friend Mrs. Wanless—the "Mary" of Chaps. XVI. and XX.—lives beside me in Newport-on-Tay, and I called the other day and had prayer with her.

She is mostly in bed now, but is pleasantly contented, and happy in the Lord.   She realises the preciousness of the Word of God, and is graciously kept by Him in peace.

> "The Lord thee keeps, the Lord thy shade
>   On thy right hand doth stay:
> The moon by night thee shall not smite,
>   Nor yet the sun by day.
>
> "The Lord shall keep thy soul, He shall
>   Preserve thee from all ill.
> Henceforth thy going out and in,
>   God keep for ever will."
>
> *Psalm* cxxi. 5–8.

"In the time of the revival," she said, "we used to meet under a tree, or on the Magdalen Green, in Dundee.

"I have much of the Bible on my heart: 'When thou passest through the waters, I will be with thee; and through the rivers, they shall not overflow thee. When thou walkest through the fire, thou shalt not be

burned, neither shall the flame kindle upon thee'
(Isa. xliii. 2). I get a great deal of comfort out of it.
One of the girls came here on Sabbath and read
to me John xiv. 3: 'I will come again, and receive
you unto Myself, that where I am, there ye may be
also.' This was great consolation to me.

"I got the news of Mr. M'Cheyne's illness on
Sabbath. I was with Mr. Nixon, the minister in
Montrose, at the time. I was coming out of the
church, when a woman stopped me and told me about
his death. They said the people prayed in groups for
him to recover; but God did not do so.

"I came and heard the funeral sermons after he
was buried. Dr. Roxburgh preached in the forenoon, and Rev. Mr. Somerville in the afternoon, and
W. C. Burns in the evening.

"I was a Sabbath-school teacher, and had ex-
Provost Hunter, Dundee, in my class, when he was
a boy. I knew Mr. Edward Caird, one of Mr.
M'Cheyne's elders; he kept a young women's class.
I was at it. I was at Mr. James Mudie's women's
class, Montrose, also, and he got me to raise the tune
at his meetings. I learned a hymn at that time,
commencing—

> "'I love the sacred book of God.'

" I learned another one which Mr. M'Cheyne used
to repeat—

> "'I asked the Lord that I might grow
> In faith, and love, and every grace,
> Might more of His salvation know,
> And seek more earnestly His face.'

"Mr. Burns was different from Mr. M'Cheyne," she added. "The former was great on law, but Mr. M'Cheyne was more on love."

Mr. William Laing of Kelleyfield writes that an old grand-aunt of his was one of M'Cheyne's members. One day he called for the old lady, rather late in the evening, and she felt he would be fatigued, and said: "I suppose it will be rather late for you to engage in prayer, Mr. M'Cheyne?" When he replied: "I hope it will never be too late to pray," and he accordingly engaged, and had prayer with the old lady.

After reading one of my sketches, the Rev. John Reid of Inverness wrote :—"Many thanks for your kindness in sending me your reminiscences of M'Cheyne. One longs for a revival here, and it increases the longing to read of what was done in the days of old.

"I think you are right in pointing out the way (see Chap. XVI.). 'Get the Bible down from the shelf, and ourselves upon our knees.' Here is a text for you, Ps. lii. 1, 'The goodness of the Lord endureth continually.'"

But all at once Mr. M'Cheyne is stricken down.

"Did you hear the news?" is the question on every side.

In a miniature way, it is in the parish and in Dundee and neighbourhood, as it would be to this nation and to the world if King Edward was laid on a bed of sickness or of death.

Meetings were held for prayer, when with deepest entreaties of affection and love his recovery was sought, and that his life might be spared to his flock, and to the Church of Christ.

"I would only be about thirteen years of age at that time," writes my friend Miss M. Sime, Dundee, to me. "There was much anxiety among the people, and they met in bands to pray for him. I remember of being at one of these meetings. An aunt of mine took me with her. It was on a Friday night.

"His doctor had said there would be a change in the morning, as it was the turn of the fever, so the meeting continued till three o'clock in the morning, when one of his servants came up to the meeting to tell us there was no change for the better; so the meeting broke up then. By nine o'clock that morning he passed away to glory.

"Most of the congregation crowded to the church in the evening. I was among them. What a meeting of weeping people! When Mr. Andrew Bonar came in, he just wept with the people. It is a scene that has never left my memory.

"I was also a witness to his funeral. I don't think there has been one like it in Dundee since. I was also present at all the funeral sermons.

"My feelings through all this was that there was a dark cloud hovering over the west end of Dundee and God speaking through the cloud. It was a long time before the feeling left me. Praise the Lord! he being dead yet speaketh.—M. SIME."

Some time ago my dear aged friend, Mr. William Robertson, Dundee, wrote me, saying, "It was very kind of you to send me one of your sketches about the old M'Cheyne days.

"I well remember him. His funeral day is still fresh in my memory. Oh! if there were only more ministers like him, the Churches would not be so empty; and the Sabbath would be better kept.

"I have a nice book," he continues, "written by Horatius Bonar, D.D., *How shall I go to God?* which I enjoy very much. I have many blessings. God has been very, very kind to me. God bless you.—W. ROBERTSON."

I have also before me a few words from old Mrs. Dewar, "Maggie's mother," as we may call her, in remembrance of dear Maggie Dewar, a life-long invalid and godly young friend, long since gone to be with Jesus:—

"I can remember my father and mother going to the church every night all the time Mr. M'Cheyne was ill; it was never shut. And such a day the funeral was to be remembered. Truly a Prince had fallen in the Church; but the dear Lord took him to be with Himself, as dear Jesus told His sorrowing disciples, 'That where I am, there ye may be also.' And it is well our dear ones are at home, and we will soon be with them.

"And it is a great responsibity to fill St. Peter's pulpit, after them that have done it before."

I cannot do better now than turn to his dear *Memoir* lying before me for some concluding sentences, as I have not come thus far without tears.

On Wednesday he felt sore and broken, and Dr. Gibson found him in fever. He said, "Shall we receive good at the hand of the Lord, and shall we not receive evil also?"

Mr. Miller of Wallacetown prayed with him, and repeated the verse, Matt. xi. 28, "Come unto Me, all ye that labour and are heavy laden, and I will give you rest," upon which Mr. M'Cheyne clasped his hands with great earnestness.

On Sabbath he said, "I am preaching the sermon that God would have me to do."

The last words he heard, and the last he seemed to understand, were those of Cowper's hymn, repeated to him by his sister, Miss Eliza M'Cheyne:

> "Sometimes a light surprises
> The Christian as he sings:
> It is the Lord who rises,
> With healing in His wings."

At one time during his delirium he said to his attendant, "Mind the text (1 Cor. xv. 58), 'Be steadfast, unmovable, always abounding in the work of the Lord, forasmuch as ye know that your labour is not in vain in the Lord.'"

Thinking he was praying for his people, he said: "You must be awakened in time, or you will be awakened in everlasting torment, to your eternal confusion."

"Thus he continued," the *Memoir* adds, "most generally engaged while the delirium lasted, either in prayer or in preaching to his people, and always apparently in happy frame till the morning of Saturday the 25th.

"On that morning, while his kind medical attendant, Dr. Gibson, stood by, Mr. M'Cheyne lifted up his hands as if in the attitude of pronouncing the blessing, and then sank down. Not a groan, or a sigh, but only a quiver of the lip, and his soul was at rest.

"His people were that evening met together in the church, and such a scene of sorrow has not often been witnessed in Scotland.   It was like the weeping for King Josiah.   Wherever the news of his departure came, every Christian countenance was darkened. Perhaps never was the death of one whose whole occupation had been preaching the everlasting Gospel more felt by all the saints of God in Scotland."

His tomb may be seen on the pathway at the north-west corner of St. Peter's Church burying-ground.   A handsome monument has been erected to his memory, bearing the following inscription :—

Erected
By his sorrowing Flock
In memory of
The Reverend ROBERT MURRAY M'CHEYNE,
First Minister of St. Peter's Church, Dundee,
Who died on the 24th day of March 1843,
In the Thirtieth Year of his Age
And Seventh of his Ministry.

———

Walking closely with God,
An example of the believers
In words, in conversation, in charity,
In spirit, in faith, in purity;
He ceased not day and night to labour
And watch for souls.
And he was honoured of God
To draw many wanderers out of darkness
Into the paths of life.

———

"Them also which sleep in Jesus will God bring with Him."

As already mentioned, I was looking on as the

funeral passed, and have often since my young days looked towards his gravestone, and have also stood beside it in deepest respect. "There is a fragrance about M'Cheyne's grave," said his friend Dr. Andrew Bonar. I think so too.

I have stood at Samuel Rutherford's grave, at John Bunyan's, Isaac Watts', Mrs. General Booth's, Wordsworth's, Benjamin Franklin's, and George Washington's; but I think no emotions were present in my mind on these occasions like as I have felt in sight of the grave of Robert Murray M'Cheyne. "The Lord gave, and the Lord hath taken away; blessed be the name of the Lord." AMEN.